JOHN CAGE (ex)plain(ed)

JOHN CAGE (ex)plain(ed)

Richard Kostelanetz

SCHIRMER BOOKS

An Imprint of Simon & Schuster Macmillan
New York

Prentice Hall International
London • Mexico City • New Delhi • Singapore
Sydney • Toronto

Schirmer Books
An Imprint of Simon & Schuster Macmillan
1633 Broadway
New York, NY 10019

Library of Congress Card Number: 95–30001

Printed in the United States of America

printing number
1 2 3 4 5 6 7 8 9 10

Library of Congress Cataloging-in-Publication Data

Kostelanetz, Richard
  John Cage (ex)plain(ed) / Richard Kostelanetz
    p. cm.
  Includes bibliographical references and index.
  ISBN 0-02-864526-X (alk. paper)
  1. Cage, John—Criticism and interpretation. I. Title
ML410.C24K73 1996
780'.92—dc20   95-30001
                                                          CIP
                                                           MN

This paper meets the requirements of ANSI/NISO Z39.48-1992 (Permanence of Paper).

For Don Gillespie and David Vaughan

There is only one content, which all great men wish to express: the longing of mankind for its future form, for an immortal soul, for dissolution into the universe—the longing of this soul for its God. This alone, though reached by many different roads and detours and expressed by many different means, is the content of the works of the great; and with all their will they yearn for it so long and desire it so intensely until it is accomplished.

—Arnold Schoenberg, Style and Idea (1950)

Contents

Part III. The Legacy

Preface

I feel as though I've been writing about John Cage my entire adult life. My first remarks about him appeared in essays published in 1964, when I was twenty-four; the first extended discussion was the 1967 *New York Times Magazine* profile that, in a revised and expanded form, appears in the opening section of this book. The most recent essay was published in 1995. In addition to writing essays wholly about Cage, I have referred to him in other essays of mine that were ostensibly devoted to other subjects. As I noted in my anthology *Writings About John Cage* (1993), the richness of Cagean commentary can be taken as a simple measure of the subject's depths; the extent of my own commentary provides a supplemental index. What is apparent now is this: Had I not discovered him early, and had I not tried to deal persistently with the critical challenges posed by his activities, my life as both a critic and an artist would have been different.

This book differs from most other writing about Cage in that it emphasizes his professional adventurousness, acknowledging not only his music but his theater, writing, radio, visual art, and much else, all reflecting a career based upon artistic (and thus artists') freedom. Though this book may be less impersonal than most arts criticism, I hope it provides an introduction to readers beginning the adventure of learning about Cage as well as information valuable to specialists.

As a distillation of three decades of critical engagements, *John Cage (ex)plain(ed)* is at once various and repetitious— various because the subject has many sides, some of which I've looked at more than once; repetitious because so many original notions (such as the conceptual weight of 4'33") must be explained again. I find myself returning to that piece even now, not only because I have new thoughts about it but also because its significance is still widely misunderstood. (For instance, it is less a "silent piece" than a "noise piece," though I among others, including Cage, have described it with the former misleading epithet.) In its variety and its departures from expository conventions, *John Cage (ex)plain(ed)* is probably more a Cagean book than a measured, continuous exposition. Some of this material has appeared in different form before, although all of it has been updated and edited.

I'm grateful to many editors for commissioning and publishing my writings on Cage; to numerous sponsors of my lectures and presentations about Cage; to Lauren Kozol and Erika Luchterhand for editing this manuscript; to Chris Potash for copyediting it; to Richard Carlin for publishing; to Cage himself, surely resting in peace, for generating so much in so many of us; and to the dedicatees for providing me with necessary information for decades (yes, decades)—the first as Cage's music publisher, the second as Merce Cunningham's archivist.

Richard Kostelanetz
New York, New York

Part 1. The Man

• method • structure • intention • discipline • notation •

indeterminacy • interpenetration • imitation • devotion •
• method • structure
circumstances • method • structure • intention • discipline
• intention • discipline
notation • indeterminacy • interpenetration • imitation •

devotion • circumstances • method • structure • intention•
• notation

discipline • notation • indeterminacy • interpenetration • imita
• indeterminacy
• devotion • circumstances • method • structure • intention •

• interpenetration
discipline • notation • indeterminacy • interpenetration •

imitation • devotion • circumstances • method • structure
• initiation

intention • discipline • notation • indeterminacy •
• devotion

interpenetration • imitation • devotion • circumstances • meth
• circumstances
• structure • intention• discipline • notation • indeterminacy •

interpenetration • imitation • devotion • circumstances • meth

• John Cage, Inventor

John Cage lived a rich life as a congenital free-spirit, making friends and establishing alliances but never joining for long any institution larger than the Merce Cunningham Dance Company. The shape of this life was important to younger people who likewise wanted to be free to do various things. He was also one of the few modern artists of whom it can be said, without dispute, that had he not existed, the development of more than one art would have been different. A true *polyartist*, Cage produced distinguished work in music, theater, literature, and visual art. As a de facto esthetician, he had a discernible influence upon the creation of music, theater, the visual arts, and, to a lesser extent, literature and social thought. His principal theme, applicable to all arts, was the denial of false authority by expanding the range of acceptable and thus employable materials, beginning with nonpitched "noises," which he thought should be heard as music "whether we're in or out of the concert hall."

Though some consider Cage an apostle of "chance," I think of him as an extremely fecund inventor who, once he transcended previous conventions, was able to realize a wealth of indubitably original constraints. The famous "prepared piano," which radically altered familiar keyboard sounds, marked merely the beginning of a career that included scrupulously alternative kinds of musical scoring, idiosyncratically structured theatrical events, and unique literary forms. Perhaps because Cage did not double back, rarely dismissing earlier works of his as no longer acceptable to him, his art remained challenging and generally unacceptable to the end. For example, in the last months of his life he completed a ninety-minute film whose visual content was a white screen violated by various shades of and shapes in gray.

When I first began following Cage's activities, three decades ago, no one so prominent, but no one, received so many persistently negative comments, not just in print but in collegial conversations. When invited to give the 1988–1989 Charles Eliot Norton lectures at Harvard, perhaps the most prestigious appointment of its kind, Cage delivered statements so barely connected that few professors returned after the initial lecture. As an anarchist from his professional beginnings, he worked, as much through example as assertion, to eliminate authority and hierarchy, even in his life, never accepting a position that might give him cultural power (as distinct from influence); never composing any work that requires an authoritarian conductor or even a lead instrumentalist who stands before a backup group. When Cage accepted the Norton position that gave him a title elevating him above the rest of humanity, I asked him what it was like being a Harvard professor. "Not much different from not being a Harvard professor," he replied, true to his politics.

Not unlike other avant-garde artists, Cage made works, in his case in various media, that are much more or much less than art used to be. Though the minimal pieces should not be slighted, in my considered opinion the greatest Cage works are his maximal compositions. *The Sonatas and Interludes for Prepared Piano* (1946–1948) is his longest and most exhaustive exploration of his first musical invention, the prepared piano. *Williams Mix* (1952) is a tape collage composed of thousands of bits, intricately fused onto several tapes that should be played simultaneously, so that the result is an abundance of sounds within only several minutes. I then like *HPSCHD* (1969), in which Cage filled a sixteen-thousand-seat basketball arena with a multitude of sounds and sights, and *Europera* (1987), which draws upon nineteenth-century European opera for musical parts, costumes, and scenarios that are distributed at random to performers in a professional opera company. Given my bias toward abundance, my favorite Cage visual art is the sequence of Plexiglas plates that became *Not Wanting to Say Anything About Marcel* (1969); my favorite Cage text, the Harvard lectures that became his longest poem, *I–VI* (1990).

In his notorious "silent piece," the superficially much, much less *4'33"* (1952), he became an avatar of conceptual art. By having the distinguished pianist David Tudor make no sounds in a concert otherwise devoted to contemporary piano music, Cage framed four minutes and thirty-three seconds of a pianist's inaction to suggest that the inadvertent sounds within the auditorium constituted the "musical" experience and, by extension, that all sounds, whether intentional or not, can be considered music. (One strain of conceptual art consists of demonstrations or statements that convey radical esthetic implications.)

Cage has also revolutionized musical scoring (even collecting an anthology of *Notations* [1969] that mostly reflects his influence), introducing graphic notations and even prose instructions in place of horizontal musical staves. The most extraordinary of his own scores is the two-volume *Song Books (Solos for Voice, 3–92* [1970] that contains, in part through length and number, an incomparable wealth of alternative performance instructions. He also belongs among the rare artists whose statements about his own work were usually more true and insightful than his critics' writings.

John Cage was one of these figures whom if he did not already exist, the philistines would need to invent. Not only were his ideas so original that they all but beg to be misunderstood and/or misinterpreted, but his was the sort of eccentricity that unenlightened minds can smugly dismiss without experiencing even a glimmer of revelation. It is true that some of his activities, which generated first-level newspaper copy, also aroused suspicions of fraudulence; however, many retrospectively unquestioned "breakthroughs" in all contemporary arts at first struck even sophisticated intelligences as suspect. Indeed, beneath Cage's comedy and his propensity for unprecedented actions were eminently serious purposes.

What makes uncomprehending criticism more irrelevant, if not more pernicious, than undiscriminating adulation is that

Cage, very much like two of his own gurus, Marshall McLuhan and Norman O. Brown, was a fount of richly imaginative ideas that cannot be rejected or accepted in toto. Quite simply, much of what he said was valuable and digestible, though also much was chaff; yet the task of winnowing poses a multifarious critical challenge that has not, in my memory, been too eagerly or thoroughly assumed.

• Fomenter of Radical Consciousness

> To be avant-garde is not merely to be different
> from what came before, but to alter radically the
> consciousness of the age.
>
> —Morris Dickstein

Although his work is so profoundly audacious that controversies about it will perhaps never cease, few can dispute that John Cage was among the most influential radical minds of his age. At the core of his originality was a continual penchant for taking positions not only far in advance of established artistic practice, including often his own activity, but also beyond the imaginative efforts that his times regarded as "avant-garde." For over fifty years, Cage worked on the frontiers of modern music and art; and as each phase of his career attracted greater support and more imitators, Cage himself progressed even further into unfamiliar territory, often further than even his most fervent admirers would go. "I like to think," he said, "that I'm outside the circle of a known universe, and dealing with things that I don't know anything about."

Everything about Cage seemed a radical departure; his music, his esthetic ideas, his personal behavior, his critical statements were all indubitably inventive. "Oh, yes, I'm devoted to the principle of originality," he once told an interviewer, "not originality in the egoistic sense, but originality in the sense of doing something which it is necessary to do. Now, obviously, the things that it is necessary to do are not those that have been done, but the ones that have not yet been done. If I have done something, then I consider it my business not to do that, but to find what must be done next." No one else would have dared announce to an audience, as well as dare to commit to print, such aphorisms as, "I have nothing to say and I am saying it and that is poetry," or "Art instead of being made by one person is a process set in motion by a group of people."

Cage's most important "compositions" were conceived to deny his intentional desires as completely as possible (although less completely than he sometimes said); and not only is each filled with a diversity of disconnected, "chance," atonal sounds, but also its major musical dimensions—amplitude (volume), duration, timbre, register—are all as unfixed, or structurally open, as the overall length of the piece.

This "indeterminate music," as Cage himself preferred to call it, was the result of an artistic evolution that was, like his esthetics, at once highly logical and faintly absurd. In the history of musical art, Cage descended from the eccentric modern tradition that abandoned nineteenth-century tonal principles and introduced natural noise as an integral component with instrumentally produced sounds; in this respect, Cage continually acknowledged the French-born American composer Edgard Varèse and, before him, Charles Ives as the artistic fathers of the radical tendencies that Cage himself later pursued. This tradition could be characterized as the "chaotic" language of contemporary music, as distinct from the mainstream language—Copland, Britten, and middle period Stravinsky—and the serial language, initiated by Arnold Schoenberg and propagated by Anton Webern, Milton Babbitt, and, in the 1950s, by Stravinsky, too.

In his earliest extant work, dating from the mid-1930s, Cage displayed huge talent for complicated rhythmic constructions; inventive organizing principles, such as a twenty-five-tone system; and distorted instrumental sounds, such as that made by immersing a gong in water. In 1937 he wrote this stunningly prophetic speculation: "I believe that the use of noise to make music will continue and increase until we reach a music produced through the aid of electrical instruments, which will make available for musical purposes any and all sounds that can be heard. Photoelectric, film, and mechanical mediums for the synthetic production of music will be explored." By 1942, Cage's *Imaginary Landscape No. 3* "combined percussion with electrical and mechanical devices, audio-frequency oscillators, variable speed turntables, variable frequency recordings [of electronic sounds made by the telephone company to test its lines], a 'generator whiner' and a buzzer," to quote the music critic Peter Yates.

In the late 1930s Cage also devised the "prepared piano," the innovation that first won him notice. Here he doctored the piano's network of strings with screws, bolts, nuts, and strips of rubber, endowing the familiar instrument with a range of unfamiliar percussive potentialities. The first famous piece for this invention was *Amores* (1943), a work which today strikes sophisticated ears as rather simplistic and conventional. Surely the most ambitious score for the prepared piano is Cage's sixty-nine-minute *The Sonatas and Interludes for Prepared Piano* (1946–1948), which seemed revolutionary at the time but now sounds like music for standard, undoctored piano that Erik Satie did a few decades before.

In addition to generating unusual noises, the prepared piano gives the performer less control over the sounds that are finally produced—bolts and nuts, alas, are not as precise as tuned strings. In contrast to the neo-Schoenbergians, who wanted a precise rationale for the placement of every note, Cage in the late 1940s continued to develop methods for minimizing his control over the aural result. Sometimes he would enumerate several possible choices posed by a compositional situation and then let the throw of dice dictate the selection. Other times he would choose his notes by first marking the miscellaneous imperfections (holes, specks, discolorations, etc.) on a piece of paper and then placing a transparent sheet over the marked paper; after duplicating these marks on the transparent sheet, he would finally trace the random dots onto musical staves.

Always opposed to the expressionistic orientation generally characteristic of mainstream composition, Cage desired "to provide a music free from one's memory and imagination." In more advanced chance work, he offered randomly produced marks on graph paper, letting the performer establish his own vertical measure for pitch and a horizontal one for duration. Sometimes he also employed the complicated and arduous dice- and coin-tossing procedures relevant to the *I Ching* (*Book of Changes*), perhaps the most ancient book of China. The result of all these techniques was a score of directions so unspecific that no two performances of the same Cage piece would ever be as recognizably alike as, say, two inept or even eccentric performances of Beethoven's Fifth Symphony.

One trouble with most of his pieces to 1952, which in retrospect seems a turning point, was that a detailed and fixed script actually produced, over a succession of performances, approximately similar results; and even the tape collage composed by chance procedures, *Williams Mix* (1952), perhaps Cage's most intricate purely aural endeavor, was offered to the world in an approximately final form. Pursuing the logic of his previous intellectual development, Cage took the esthetic leaps that made his music even more indeterminate in both conception and execution, so that each performance of a piece would be hugely different from all the others. In *Winter Music* (1957), for instance, the score consists of clusters of notes irregularly displayed across its twenty pages; these may be "used in whole or part by a pianist or shared by two to twenty [performers] to provide a program of agreed-upon length." The instructions continue, "The notation in space may be interpreted as to time. . . . Resonances, both aggregates and individual notes of them, may be free in length. . . . Dynamics are free." All the traditional dimensions of music are by intention free, free, free.

Perhaps the single most revolutionary piece in the Cage canon is *4'33"*, pronounced "Four Minutes and Thirty-three Seconds." In its original performance, the well-known pianist David Tudor came to the piano and sat still, except for three silent motions with his hands, for the prescribed duration. On the surface, this is, of course, just nothing; but precisely because the presence of David Tudor and the concert-going audience made this a situation from which musical sound was expected, the dramatized inference was that the piece's "music" consisted of all the sounds that happened to be audible in the performance hall during the time period of *4′33″*. As some, if not most, of these accidental noises came from the audience, the spectators could be counted among the performance's musicians. As "silence" signifies the absence of intentional sound, Cage called the resulting piece "non-intentional" music.

Not only did *4′33″* contribute to musical history by bringing the chaotic musical tradition to one "logical" end point, but also it belongs among those rare modern pieces that are important less for the explicit experiences they offer than the extraordinary artistic ideas their circumstances imply. As a stunt invested with meaning, this piece, as well as Cage himself, suggests not only that all sounds, in any combination, are justifiable components of music—actually a position that Cage insisted dates back to Claude Debussy and the origins of modernism—but also that unintentional noises, regardless of their quality, are as valid for music as sounds intentionally produced. Indeed, most of Cage's own pieces since *4′33″* were designed to incorporate unintentional or "found" sounds into their aural field; but the ultimate implication of *4′33″* was that anything is possible in art, including (and here is the radical leap) *nothing at all.* "I have nothing to say and I am saying it and that is poetry."

In retrospect, however, Cage regarded even this extreme piece as needlessly conservative, not only because it has three "movements," as indicated by the performer's silent gyrations, but also because it occurs within a fixed time and an enclosed space. Because silence, which was the surface content of *4′33″*, can never be absolute, then the "music" of that piece, which is to say unintentional noise, is with us all the time, if we attune ourselves to perceive it. In that case, the act of experiencing

4′33″ prepares a listener for the unprecedented perception of all the music in the environment. "If you want to know the truth of the matter," Cage once told me, with a twinkle composed one half of enthusiasm, the other half of irony, "The music I prefer, even to my own and everything, is what we hear if we are just quiet." Accepting the implications of all his actions, Cage deduced that the most agreeable art is not only just like life—it is life. In other words, 4′33″ is not only a work of art, but a statement about esthetic experience. As such, it illustrates the art historian George Kubler's classic observation, in *The Shape of Time* (1962), that "The work of many artists often comes closer to philosophical speculation than most esthetic writings."

Following his own deductions, Cage gladly admitted that he intellectually programmed himself out of a musical career; still, he continued to create indeterminate compositions, partly to expose his audience to the aurally chaotic character of the environment, but mostly because, he said, of a promise he made in the early 1930s to Arnold Schoenberg to devote his entire life to music in exchange for the elder composer's free lessons. Cage also took from the Indian philosopher Ananda K. Coomaraswamy the suggestive principle that "art imitates nature in its manner of operation." The result is a scrupulously discontinuous aural art, with no climaxes, no resolutions, no regular beats, no consistent tonality, no aural concurrences, no discernible beginnings, no definite ends—as random and haphazard as life. "Each sound is heard for itself," the critic Jill Johnston commented, "and does not depend for its value on its place within a system of sounds." *Imaginary Landscape No. 4* is composed for twelve radios and twenty-four performers, one for each station-selecting dial, the other for each volume-control knob. Although Cage offers his performers a fixed script, he obviously has no control over what the radios will blare, if they play anything at all. At minimum, as Peter Yates once quipped, Cage "emancipated music from its notes."

The score of *Atlas Eclipticalis* (1961–1962), which Cage composed by transferring the patterns of stars from an atlas to sheets of music paper, offers eighty-six instrumental parts "to be played in whole or part, for any duration, in any ensemble, chamber or orchestral, of the above performers [an eccentric assortment]; with or without *Winter Music*." Here and elsewhere, Cage was not adverse to performing two of his pieces simultaneously; among the more exciting combinations is the singer Cathy Berberian's recording of *Aria* (1958) with *Fontana Mix* (1958). Regarding records of Cage's work, one should add that, because the current technology of recording instruments can capture only one "rendition" of an indeterminate score, all available records or tapes of Cage's post-1952 pieces inevitably compromise his ultimate esthetic purposes.

Rozart Mix (1965), originally composed for the Rose Art Museum at Brandeis University, employs six live performers, thirteen tape machines, and a pile of at least eighty-eight tape loops (where the two ends of a piece of recording tape are glued together) of varying lengths. Cage specified the unusually large number, he explained, "to make sure that the performers wouldn't select tapes only of their favorite pieces." At the beginning of *Rozart Mix*, each of the performers picks a tape from the pile of loops and places it on the machine; when a tape breaks or gets tangled, she or he replaces it with another tape chosen from the pile: "What you want, you see, is to get a physically confused situation." Although the machines are tuned to various amplitudes, the piece itself is a paralyzingly loud chaos of sounds. As frequently happens at Cage's concerts, unenlightened spectators trickle out after every cacophonous climax. At the premiere performance, refreshments were served when the audience dwindled to twelve; and the piece terminated, by prearrangement, when the last spectator left the Rose Art Museum, approximately two hours after *Rozart Mix* began. (The hors d'oeuvre to this main course consisted of Cage's munching a sandwich whose sound was picked up by contact microphones strategically distributed around his face, so that excruciatingly loud crunching noises penetrated every nook of the hall.)

Cage often characterized his intentions as "purposeful purposelessness." He also described his art as closer to action than creation: "Art instead of being an object made by one person is a process set in motion by a group of people." One should add that purposeful purposelessness is considerably different from purposeless purposelessness, just as orderly disorder—the character of Cage's art—differs from disorderly disorder. For those reasons, an experienced ear can instantly identify Cage as the author of his pieces; in the choice of materials and guidelines lies his taste.

He was known to become visibly upset if the skeleton of his piece, as distinct from the detail, lost its predetermined shape. "The rules of the game," quipped Peter Yates, "determine the nature of the play and the shape of the end product." In that his later pieces are usually extravagant in character, open in time, indeterminate in action, and yet fixed in space (the enclosed performance area), they are closer to staged happenings than musical theater, although more than one critic has praised them as the most interesting and valid species of American "opera."

Over the years, Cage published a modest number of eccentrically conceived essays, mostly in music and art magazines. The earliest of these he collected into a volume appropriately titled *Silence* (1961), dedicated "To Whom It May Concern." It remained his single most influential book. Indeed, from the mid-1950s he developed a concentrated interest in prose forms, first overcoming certain affectations that plagued his earlier style and then striving for original ways to express his ideas and illustrate his esthetic principles. *Indeterminacy* (1959), recorded on a Folkways record, is an imaginative esthetic demonstration in the form of a lecture; so is "Where Are We Going? and What Are We Doing?" (1961) as well as

"Talk I" (1965), among other word-pieces. The last is reprinted in Cage's second collection, *A Year from Monday* (1967), which also contains his stunning collection of random anecdotes and radical speculations, the three-part "Diary: How to Improve the World (You Will Only Make Matters Worse)" (1965–67). This set of related pieces is composed under a system of self-imposed constraints that paradoxically freed him from conventional ways of putting words together; the result is a rhythmic word-form somewhere between prose and poetry, though closer to the latter. "Poetry is not prose," he once wrote, "not by reason of its content or ambiguity but by reason of its allowing musical elements (time, sound) to be introduced into the world of words."

Cage led a vagabond life, as his physical movement paralleled his esthetic adventure. He was born September 5, 1912, in Los Angeles, the son of an inventor and electrical engineer, John Cage Sr., whose gasoline-engine submarine temporarily established, in the year of John Jr.'s birth, the world's record for staying underwater. Young Cage became valedictorian of his Los Angeles high school class and entered nearby Pomona College just before his seventeenth birthday; however, somewhat appalled, he said, at the academic regimentation of individual curiosity, he soon dropped out, traveling for over a year through Europe, where he dabbled in architecture and painting, before returning to Los Angeles. Once home, he decided to concentrate on music, studying briefly with Henry Cowell and Adolph Weiss. He later convinced Arnold Schoenberg, the Viennese composer who had recently emigrated to Los Angeles, to give him free lessons in exchange for the promise mentioned before. Despite Schoenberg's generosity, Cage found the European serial techniques uncongenial, while the several extant stories of Schoenberg's real opinion of Cage are contradictory.

In the late 1930s Cage took a job as resident accompanist at the Cornish School in Seattle, Washington, where he first met the dancer and choreographer Merce Cunningham, then a student of acting, who was to become Cage's closest friend and professional associate. In 1937 he married Xenia Andreyevna Kashevaroff, the Alaskan daughter of a Russian Orthodox priest; they lived together for about a decade, later divorcing. In 1942 Cage taught music at László Moholy-Nagy's Chicago Bauhaus, then called the Institute of Design, taking various odd jobs to supplement his meager teaching income. The following year the Cages came to New York with a few dollars in hand and a tenuous invitation to stay with Max Ernst and his wife, the art collector Peggy Guggenheim. Thanks to the aid of newly acquired friends, Cage managed the following year to present at the Museum of Modern Art the crucial concert that initiated his reputation as a controversial force on the New York musical scene.

Unable in those days to support himself through musical activities alone, or to earn a permanent teaching position, Cage lived modestly in sparsely furnished rooms on Monroe Street on New York's Lower East Side. He ran through a gamut of jobs—dishwasher, library researcher, accompanist to dancers, freelance music instructor, and art director of a textile company, among them. Remembering the example of Schoenberg's generosity, he gave free lessons to those who could not afford to pay. Not until the 1960s was he able to live as a composer on royalties from his music and writings, visiting professorships at the Universities of Cincinnati, Illinois, and elsewhere, and an endless number of lectures and performances. By that time being John Cage had, in fact, become quite lucrative. The coterie of his vociferous admirers, merely a handful in the 1940s, had swelled to a considerable populace.

Cage continued to live alone as frugally as ever, spending the middle part of his adult life living in an artist's community about an hour north of New York City. But even this country habitat was simple. His house was a minuscule, glass-walled two-and-a-half-room cottage on top of a treacherously rocky path; between his two small rooms (each about twenty feet by ten) lay a narrow utility core, where Cage usually cooked for himself. In the back room was one all-purpose table (eating, writing, and talking over), a small bed, and piles of reading matter. Cage's final residence was a large New York City loft above what was once a major department store, shared with Merce Cunningham; its large windows made it an ideal space for a large number and variety of potted plants.

In public situations, Cage emitted an aura of youthful optimism—"a sunny disposition" is his own phrase for it—and as his old friend Peter Yates observed, "Around him everyone laughs." Cage's slight build, his unfluctuating scalp line, his thick brown hair that was slow to gray, all made him look considerably younger than his years; only the deep lines running down the sides of his face betrayed his age. Actually, Cage offered the world two distinct faces, one hardly resembling the other. The "serious" face was long and narrow, with wide and attentive brown eyes, unusually long ears, and vertical lines sloping down to his heavy jaw; in contrast, Cage's "comic" face, which graced most of his public pictures, was horizontal in structure, his wide mouth exposing two rows of teeth, his eyes nearly closed.

Cage was immensely gregarious, talking freely and laughing easily; contagiously enthusiastic, he seemed blessed with a limitless capacity for getting people to do him favors. Also a great theatrical presence, thanks to a sharp sense of timing, he could upstage nearly anyone, including the entire Merce Cunningham troupe. When he confronted audiences, his answers and examples, gestures and jokes came easily to him, in much the same tone and form night after night, place after place. As a matter of principle he refused to indulge in argument, even in the presence of those he considered his antagonists; yet he could sometimes be outrageously nasty about people who were not present. As persuasion was among his primary purposes, Cage often seemed all but Jesuitical, particularly with possible skeptics, continually making sounds and gestures intended to elicit agreement. His most distressing habit was name-dropping, which he did so compulsively that sometimes rather trivial ideas got attached to awesomely eminent sources. He smoked cigarettes through a filter for many years, and was forever changing his taste in alcoholic drinks. Especially in the 1960s, when I first met him, he morally objected to the use of drugs, which he called "dopes," for the same reason he opposed Art: both promise transcendence from mundane life. Cage's high-pitched, raspy voice was instantly recognizable, and his most serious talk seemed closer to philosophy than music or art criticism.

What makes Cage's esthetic position so revolutionary is that, in theory at least, it completely discounts the traditional purposes of composing and even the importance of the composer. As Cage would have it, music is everywhere, and everywhere *is* music—nature's natural noise—if only the listener is prepared to hear it. Therefore, if the composer has any function at all, it should be, Cage said, teaching people to keep attuned to all the implicit music that their environment offers. Following the logic of this position, he admitted that solipsism characterizes the experience of both everyday life and indeterminate music; and, because each person hears something individual, everyone is his or her own composer, putting sound together, in the act of attentive listening. The music most appropriate to our time is that which allows each listener to compose an individual experience, his argument continued. Therefore, too, Cage regarded a performance of a Beethoven quartet as "no longer what Beethoven wrote but everything else I happen to hear at that time. We must take intentional material, like Beethoven, and turn it to non-intention."

If music is all sounds, whether intentional or not, then theater, by Cage's analogy, consists of all the impressions that meet the eye and ear, which is to say that theater is as constantly available to the perceptive sensibility as music: "Theater takes place all the time, wherever one is. And art simply facilitates persuading one this is the case." In the mid-1950s Cage recognized that his own compositions were, in performance, as much theater as music. In *Theatre Piece* (1960) he extended an implication of *Music Walk* (1958) and provided instructions for the indeterminate movements of people as well as the generation of sounds.

Actually, Cage was continually involved with theater. Not only did he serve for over three decades as the musical director of Merce Cunningham's dance company, but back in the summer of 1952 he staged what was probably the first American "happening," at Black Mountain College in North Carolina. Furthermore, the classes he taught in "music composition" at the New School, from 1956 to 1958, included several students who later became creators of the happenings theater: Allan Kaprow, Dick Higgins, Jackson Mac Low, and George Brecht. Cage remained in many ways the esthetic father, as well as a foremost practitioner, of the art of nonliterary performance that I have elsewhere called "The Theater of Mixed Means." Indeed, his own best theatrical pieces were extravagant in materials, scrupulously chaotic in effect, tasteful in scale, and idiosyncratic in identity; to many polyliterate critics, including myself, Cage's performances were generally more valid and laudatory as theatrical spectacle than as purely aural (that is, musical) experience.

In the late 1940s Cage attended D. T. Suzuki's lectures on oriental religion at Columbia University; from then on he considered himself a devotee of Zen Buddhism. (He recalled that when he told his mother about receiving a one-year appointment at Wesleyan University, she replied, "Do they know you're a Zen Buddhist?") One Zen tenet that Cage found congenial is the total acceptance of perceptual reality—the music around us all the time—that Cage described as "perfectly satisfactory." "We open our eyes and ears, seeing life each day excellent as it is." Such a position, he admitted, should completely negate the exercise of discriminatory taste and the expression of evaluative judgments; but just as he did not devote his professional career to innumerable performances of 4'33", so he never was able to flush away the critical sense he acquired as a young artist. In *Silence* he writes admiringly of a Japanese Roshi who accompanied him to a New York dinner, after which the host and hostess insisted upon singing arias from a third-rate Italian opera in fourth-rate voices. "I was embarrassed and glanced toward the Roshi to see how he was taking it," Cage remembers. "The expression on his face was absolutely beatific."

Indeed, Cage was always embarrassed to find that his own attitudes and practices never caught up with his espoused positions; many of his apparent contradictions, upon which his critics feast, stem from this discrepancy. In theory he was opposed to critical judgments, explaining, "They are destructive to our proper business, which is curiosity and awareness." He elaborated: "Why waste time by focusing upon these questions of value and criticism and so forth and by making negative statements. We must exercise our time positively. . . . The big thing to do actually is to get yourself into a situation where you use your experience, no matter where you are. . . . How are you going to use this situation if you are there? This is the big question."

In rebuttal I once suggested that, no matter how attentive we are, certain extrinsic experiences are intrinsically richer than others. Only partially assimilating my objection, Cage continued, "I've noticed that I can pick up anything in the way of a periodical or a newspaper—anything—and use it . . . in the content sense, in terms of its relevance to positive action now. Now let's ask this kind of question: Which is more valuable—to read *The New York Times* which is a week old or to read Norman O. Brown's *Love's Body*? If we face this issue squarely, we'll see that there's no difference." Nonetheless, he rarely read newspapers.

In practice, however, Cage frequently made rather decisive critical judgments, as he preferred art that is formally variable and open rather than constant and fixed, and as discontinuously complex as life itself. For instance, he esthetically objected to nearly all contemporary music—both mainstream and serial, both jazz and rock—because the results are fixed objects for contemplation rather than processes that expose us to life. He said he generally preferred theater to concerts, because it "more than music resembles nature." Rather than hear one jazz band pound a steady beat, he would prefer to listen to several combos playing in different tempi at once. If pressed, Cage would admit that evaluative standards often informed the choices he made in his daily activity. "When I am making them," he mused, "I'm annoyed that I am doing so."

"In Zen they say: If something is boring after two minutes, try it for four. If still boring, try it for eight, sixteen, thirty-two, and so on. Eventually one discovers that it's not boring but very interesting." Elsewhere in *Silence*, he wrote that boredom can often "induce ideas." Not only are his esthetics quoted to rationalize much that is repetitious, unarticulated, and interminable in recent art, but surely those arduous chance procedures must cause boring experiences; yet in conversation I more than once heard Cage compromise his position by dismissing a certain activity in life as "a terrible bore."

Although Cage continued to author new pieces each year and perform those earlier works whose aleatoric processes he still regarded as valid, his passions became more varied. In the mid-1950s he developed an interest in mushrooms, not only collecting various species but also accumulating a huge library of relevant literature. "I once thought I should like to be a botanist, because I felt that that field, unlike music, would have an absence of strife. I have since discovered otherwise." For a short period in 1960 he supplied New York's posh Four Seasons restaurant with edible fungi; and in 1962 he became a founding officer of the New York Mycological Society. In a Zenish explanation, he once linked his two primary enthusiasms, music and mushrooms, to the fact that they appear adjacent to each other in most dictionaries.

Sustaining his youthful interest in visual art, Cage made intricately conceived and exquisitely executed scores, which in 1958 he exhibited at New York's Stable Gallery. "They are set down in a complex system of numbers, notes, letters, and geometrical formations," wrote Dore Ashton, then an art critic at *The New York Times*, "and each page has a calligraphic beauty quite apart from its function as a musical composition." In the late 1960s Cage compiled a rich book of modern compositional notation—an anthology of manuscripts by the major modern composers—partially to benefit the Foundation for Contemporary Performance Arts, which he helped establish.

In the late 1960s Cage became an enthusiastic devotee and publicist of an eccentric strain of avant-garde radical social thought. Long an individualist anarchist (a logical analog to his esthetic notion that every person is a composer), Cage propagated a mix of ideas taken mostly from Marshall McLuhan, Buckminster Fuller (an old friend from their days together at Black Mountain), Norman O. Brown, and Robert Theobald. In general, Cage forecast the time when autonomous technology would achieve an economy of unbounded abundance, which would eventually ensure everyone a guaranteed annual income, regardless of whether she or he was able to work or not. Such an economic revolution, he believed, would necessitate further social and psychological revolutions, making play, rather than work, the dominant motive of human activity. Thus, he regarded chance composition and happenings performance, which are closer to inspired play than hard-nosed work, as harbingers of the new age. His later writings seemed explorations in interdisciplinary thought, much as his later performance pieces are explorations in intermedia art.

Cage's eminence stems less from his artistic works as such, which even some of his more devoted admirers find tiresome, than the impact of his persuasive ideas and friendship upon scores of artists, musicians, theater directors, critics, and choreographers. Indeed, no single figure in the American arts influenced so many first-rank creative minds as profoundly, perhaps because no one was as determined as Cage to liberate all contemporary art from all irrelevant strictures and boundaries. Not only through his occasional lectures to gatherings of abstract expressionists during the early 1950s but also through his close personal friendships with both Jasper Johns and Robert Rauschenberg, Cage influenced many tendencies in contemporary painting, including the penchant for mixing artistic media, as in Rauschenberg's "combines," and the rationale informing "minimal" painting and sculpture, as well as the elegant representation of popular images. "That atmosphere [behind pop art]," writes the art critic Barbara Rose, "was generated mainly by the composer John Cage."

Cage also influenced the more advanced tendencies in contemporary dance, not only through his close association with Merce Cunningham and, at various times, Jean Erdman, but also because one of his own composition pupils, Robert Dunn, taught the classes that inspired one of the most radical developments in post-Cunningham dance—the collection of adventurous performance activities of the Judson Church movement. Cage's influence also helped raze the lines that traditionally separated one art from another, providing precedents for works that straddle traditional domains—happenings, environmental sculptures, visual poems, and so on. "Now we have such a marvelous loss of boundaries," he told me, "that your criticism of a happening could be a piece of music or a scientific experiment or a trip to Japan or a trip to your local shopping market."

In addition, Cage fathered an entire school of American composition, which includes, among others, Earle Brown and Morton Feldman, James Tenney and Christian Wolff. Influenced in part by Cage's example, the European composers Pierre Boulez and Karlheinz Stockhausen introduced aleatoric elements into their previously fixed pieces. Even the contrived chaos of musically sophisticated rock groups seems ultimately, though circuitously, indebted to Cage's forays into aural possibility; for who else dares say that anything is possible in music, including sheer cacophony and/or nothing at all. Indeed, because Cage's ideas are so relevant, so multifarious, so revolutionary, so pervasive, it is all but impossible to talk about what is interesting in contemporary art without mentioning his name or considering his extraordinary radical ideas.

• Cunningham/Cage

Merce Cunningham and John Cage—sometimes they were separate, sometimes together. They began separately, Cage in Los Angeles in 1912, Cunningham in Centralia, Washington, around 1919. They first met in Seattle, in the late 1930s at the Cornish School, where Cage was a dance-class pianist and Cunningham a student. They came together again in New York in the early 1940s and, ever since their first joint concert in 1944, worked together, pursuing, individually and together, similar esthetic ideas and artistic lives. Each began his own career as a favored child of a reigning establishment, and each rejected that establishment, in turn to be rejected by it, before successfully forging a professional identity based upon extreme innovation.

Historically, Merce Cunningham is best seen as epitomizing the third generation of modern-dance choreography. The first generation, led by Isadora Duncan, rejected the tone and devices of classical ballet, with its fixed vocabulary of positions and movements, and put the dancer's feet flat on the floor and used freely formed gestures that appeared more expressive of human emotions than the strict conventions of ballet. Duncan and her contemporaries established a choreographic tradition that has developed apart not only from ballet but from folk dance, ethnic dance, social dance, jazz dance, chorus lines, and vaudeville dance.

The second generation of modern dance introduced more definite vocabularies of movement (Martha Graham, for instance, favoring contractions and releases). Works such as *Appalachian Spring* (Graham) or *The Moor's Pavanne* (by José Limón), customarily had particular subjects that evoked a plot and/or depended upon a familiar literary allusion. Like Duncan before them, these choreographers danced on standard theatrical stages to conventionally tonal music, the rhythm of their movements relating to the predictable musical beat; and their typical gestures served to mime identifiable emotions or meanings.

By the time he first met Cunningham, Cage had dropped out of college and had lived in Europe and in New York, where he studied with serial composers. Once back home in Los Angeles, he asked to study with Arnold Schoenberg, who had emigrated there. Though Schoenberg thought enough of Cage to give him free lessons, he eventually told the young man he lacked talent for harmony. In the sort of gesture that seems at once typical of avant-garde artists and indicative of his determination, Cage decided nonetheless to compose music that eschewed harmony. (Given this incapacity, it is scarcely surprising that Cage disparaged Stravinsky's neoclassicism, which was influential in the 1930s.) Initially he worked with percussion instruments, then with a prepared piano (which transformed that traditional musical instrument into a percussion ensemble). He began to explore electronic sound generation, at first through record turntables whose speed could be modulated; eventually, transferring his allegiance from Schoenberg to the chaotic tradition of Charles Ives and Edgard Varèse, Cage thought of composing from sounds heard on the street.

In the late 1940s Cage studied with the Japanese philosopher D. T. Suzuki and discovered an application of Zen Buddhism to art—the acceptance of all sounds, apart from intention and apart from structure, as equally valid. His most conclusive demonstration of this principle is 4'33" (1952). As no intentional sound was made by the pianist, Cage's polemical implication was that all the miscellaneous sounds occurring within that time frame constituted "the music." From this principle, for instance, follows his use of chance procedures, and the *I Ching*, to make compositional decisions that discount expressionistic motives and personal taste. To the end of his life, Cage insisted that 4'33" was his most important single work, as well as the most influential upon his subsequent compositional thinking.

Once a principal performer in the Graham company, Merce Cunningham had by the late 1940s moved outside the bounds of his profession. Not only were his performances with Cage unreviewed, they were frequently excluded from "series" anthologies where they deservedly belonged. Or, included in a series one year, he was excluded the next, "with a note I thought impolite." Cage's musical career traversed a similar wayward road well into the 1960s. The reason for their divergence was artistic rather than personal; for at issue was not just a difference in "style," but Cunningham's and Cage's radical departures in compositional approach. Because their works "broke the rules" and thus were different in more ways than the dance and music worlds could understand, both men, separately and together, were widely dismissed as "unserious" or "absurd."

Both Cunningham and Cage were also reacting against the predominant esthetic thinking of the post–World War II years—Suzanne K. Langer's philosophy of art as symbolic representation. (It was taught to me in college as late as 1960.) The function of art, she wrote, is "the creation of forms symbolic of human feeling." The artist thus endeavors to create structures that present "semblances" of familiar emotions. If the symbolic presentation is true to a form of a certain feeling, then this formal abstraction will not only give esthetic pleasure by itself, it will also function to instigate that particular feeling in the spectator. The intellectual achievement of Langer's esthetics was a richly supported theory of art-as-emotion that avoided traditional schemes of expression and individual personality on the one hand, and explicit universal myth on the other. At the time it seemed perfectly relevant to the representational music of Aaron Copland, the programmatic dance of Martha Graham, the poetry of T. S. Eliot, and the new postcubist abstract painting. However, Langerian esthetics did not relate to Cunningham/Cage, who have little taste for symbolism or ulterior meanings.

Not only for music but for his visual art and writing as well, Cage evolved a radical esthetic of nonfocused, nonhierarchical fields without definite beginnings or ends. Because he was less interested in relationships and cohering structures than in isolated sounds, his works tend to be constellations of parts, none of them more important, more climactic, or more cohesive than any other. Though his pieces necessarily begin and end, neither the opening element nor the closing element makes a firm impression. The radicalness of this kind of structuring should not be underestimated; for whereas classical notions of artistic form deal with centering and focus and favor arclike shapes that organize emphases and have firm beginnings and ends, Cage, as well as Cunningham, did something else.

Cunningham meanwhile radically reworked several dimensions of dancemaking—not only the function of gestures but the articulation of time and the use of space. First of all, he eschewed the idea of movement as meant to tell a story or articulate an emotion. Second, whereas most choreographers posited a central theme that informed all the parts, which in turn reinforced the initial concept, Cunningham's works are assembled from disparate, independently created materials that remain perceptibly separate and yet artistically complementary in the final performance. (His "Events" extend this radical structural bias in assembling, fresh for each occasion, passages originally composed for different dances.) Third, whereas most ballet and even most modern dance has a front and a back, Cunningham's works are designed to be seen from all sides; and though theatrical custom has forced him to do most of his performances on a proscenium stage (which has an open front), his pieces have also been successfully performed in gymnasiums and museums. Much as Cage built upon his personal insufficiencies with harmony, so Cunningham's choreography depended first upon his tight-jointedness—he could leap but he could not stretch—and then upon insufficiencies in interpersonal communication and in following a plot.

Because their artistic moves were ends in themselves, rather than parts of intended structures or, worse, vehicles of emotional representation, Cunningham and Cage freed themselves to explore the limitless possibilities of their materials: sound, image, and language for Cage, human movement and theatrical platforms for Cunningham. Capitalizing on the freedoms they had given themselves, each has been doggedly prolific and incomparably inventive. Assimilating Cage's interests in autonomy and chance, Cunningham defied tradition by allowing parts of the dancer's body to function disjunctively and nonsynchronously. Once, in *Untitled Solo* (1953), he listed the movable parts of the body and enumerated their possible actions before tossing dice to determine theoretically possible combinations that he might be reluctant to try on his own initiative. As exploration rather than, say, refinement has been their mutual ideal, Cunningham then took months to test all his aleatory results, until he found, after repeatedly trying, that a few hypothetical combinations were simply physically impossible.

Because his art, as well as Cage's, scrupulously eschews specific subjects or stories, Cunningham's dancers avoid dramatic characterizations for nonparticularized roles, which is to say that they always play themselves and no one else. Because they avoid the traditional structure of theme and variation, the dominant events within a given work seem to proceed at an irregular, unpredictable pace; their temporal form is, metaphorically, lumpy. "It's human time," Cunningham once explained, "which can't be too slow or too fast, but includes various time possibilities. I like to change tempos."

Their most radical idea was the separate creation of sound and choreography, so that dancers would not hear the music until just before the performance; for as early as 1939, Cage advocated "the simultaneous composition of both dance and music." Cunningham has always identified Cage as the principal influence upon his work, "because of his ideas about the possibilities of sound and time and the separate identities of music and dance."

Since Cunningham's nonsymbolic movements are meant to be appreciated apart from larger structures, his dance demands not the empathy of the spectator but, as Cage once explained, "your faculty of kinesthetic sympathy. It is this faculty we employ when, seeing the flight of birds, we ourselves, by identification, fly up, glide and soar." Of Cage's music, the dance critic Jill Johnston once wrote, "Each sound is heard for itself and does not depend for its value on its place within a system of sounds. Similarly, a typical Cunningham movement is a series of isolated actions, and the connection is simply that of sequence or juxtaposition, or whatever the observer wishes to make out of it." From Cunningham/Cage collaborations have come the currently popular customs of keeping apart those elements that might normally be expected to coincide, or of simultaneously offering materials that otherwise have nothing to do with one another. Their great, much-imitated idea was presentational noncongruence.

Both also challenged the traditional hierarchies of artistic practice, avoiding the format of "leader and chorus" which is typical of most music for large ensembles and much modern dance. Their performance ensembles tend to be companies of equals, who perform without a visible conductor, whose various members dominate at different times; and rather than looking and dressing alike, as is customary in most performing companies, these collaborators accentuate individuality in both appearance and activity. Unison activity, when used, is rarely sustained, as individual dancers move at different speeds and individual musicians play at different tempi, often simultaneously. In the end, what at first seems diffused and inscrutable in their work is quite comprehensible, providing one does not strive too hard to find "meanings" that are not there. What you see or hear is what there is.

Throughout the history of their collaboration, Cage always seemed the more "offensive," his egregiously dissonant scores distracting attention from the dance as well as offending "music lovers" even more than Cunningham's art disturbs dance regulars. I remember a performance at Lincoln Center's Philharmonic Hall in 1963, as part of a subscription series with more conservative choreographers. At the time, a typical Cagean piece consisted of silences punctuated by earsplitting amplified cacophonies (or vice versa). After every resounding crescendo, several spectators arose to march, disgusted, to the exits, effectively reducing the uptown audience to true Cunningham aficionados. It was a sight. Days later, the *New York Times* critic suggested, not unreasonably, that Cunningham might hence succeed with the Philharmonic audience if he dumped Cage. In *The Village Voice*, Jill Johnston, its dance critic at the time, responded that such bowdlerization would be comparable to "the Bible without God." In truth, Cage could have written more, and probably earned more, had he not spent so much of his life accompanying Cunningham.

One reason Cunningham appears less "free" is his acceptance of limitations, initially in the human body but also in the responsibilities of directing a company of full-time dancers. About the former limitation he once told an interviewer, "With dancing we're locked into the fact that it's the human body doing the action. There are two legs; the arms move a certain number of ways; the knees only bend forwards. That remains your limit." This sense of circumscription, along with a more pronounced taste for the exquisite, accounts for why most of us think Cunningham less radical than Cage. If Cage had been a choreographer, he would, by contrast, probably have thought of how to transcend those limits and—let me speculate further— thus envision theatrical performances for puppets or robots. After all, Cage pioneered composition with audiotape, which was likewise about realizing acoustically with technology what could not be done with physically limited live performers.

Initially both men found their most loyal audience not among composers and dancers but among visual artists. The painter Elaine de Kooning tells the story that just before a 1954

Cunningham performance, the critic Harold Rosenberg screamed in his booming voice, "Here it is almost curtain time and the Lassaws [the sculptor Ibram and his wife] aren't here yet." Then to top this joke, Rosenberg added, with utter confidence that his crack would not be misunderstood, "There's a stranger in the third row. Throw him out." So chummy was his audience that by the mid-1950s, Cunningham once told me, half its faces were familiar. Back in 1966, Cage told the art critic Irving Sandler, "Any experimental musician in the twentieth century has had to rely on painters, because they were the lively changers of art to begin with." In the early 1960s Cunningham's principal patrons included the freshly successful painters Jasper Johns and Robert Rauschenberg.

Together and separately, Cage and Cunningham rank among the most influential artists of their time, affecting not only their own arts but, more significantly perhaps, others as well. In his 1971 memoir of the poet Frank O'Hara, John Ashbery recalls back in the early 1950s a Cage "piano work lasting over an hour and consisting, as I recall, entirely of isolated, autonomous tone-clusters struck seemingly at random all over the keyboard." The effect upon those poets, then still in their twenties, was "further, perhaps for us ultimate proof not so much of 'Anything goes' but 'Anything can come out.'"

I see the subsequent influence of Cunningham and Cage in the unfettered exploration of materials thought unsuitable for art, whether noises in music or junk in sculpture; in extended uninflected discontinuous structures, whether in nonsyntactic prose or in dance; and in performances whose parts are not obviously complementary. (A richly varied multimedia exhibition could be assembled of work reflecting their initiative.) Perhaps the surest test of their influence is the general belief that had they not done what they did, recent American arts would have been drastically different.

Cunningham and Cage collaborated for over forty years, in one of the richest continuing relationships in all modern art.

To each came well-earned, indisputable rewards—a Kennedy Center Honor and a MacArthur Award for Cunningham, so many commissions for Cage that he finally needed to retire from his traditional job as music director of the dance company. Unique though each is, their most extraordinary achievement was surely their collaboration, not only rich in quality and influence but sustained in duration.

• John Cage, Polyartist

I.

John Cage was not just a composer who wrote or a writer who composed, to cite two familiar formulations, but a new modern species, a *polyartist*, which is my coinage for someone who excels at two or more nonadjacent arts. This term, *polyartist*, is magical, because, like all good critical terms, it not only clarifies a concern that is otherwise inchoate, but it dispenses with false issues and irrelevant caveats. To call Cage a polyartist is to say that he excelled at more than one nonadjacent art or, more precisely, that he was a master of several unrelated arts. The principal qualifier in my definition is *nonadjacent*. By contrast, sculpture and painting are adjacent visual arts, so someone excelling at both painting and sculpture is not a polyartist; similarly, poetry and fiction are adjacent arts. So are photography and film. However, painting and poetry are not adjacent; music and fiction are not.

In Cage's work in music and visual art, in theater and in writing, we find a pattern of unity amid all the activities. The generative idea involves nonfocused, nonhierarchical agglomerations that lack definite beginnings and ends and that—in contrast to classical ideas of form—avoid climax and cohesion. There are glimmers of this alternative structure in his early music, such as *First Construction (in Metal)* (1939) in which the emphases come so thick and fast that the entire work is finally nonclimactic in overall form. To get a sense of the difference between classical structure and Cagean structure, contrast J. S. Bach's *Well-Tempered Clavier* with a comparable exhaustive Cagean piece for a comparable instrument, *The Sonatas and Interludes for Prepared Piano* (1946–1948). Bach's short pieces are traditionally structured, with clear beginnings and ends as well as cumulative linear interweavings;

Cage's intrinsically autonomous uninflected passages represent, by contrast, a radical departure from such classical forming.

However, not until the early 1950s did Cage fully realize his characteristic structure—not only in *4'33"* (1952), the notorious silent piece in which the inferred aural experience must likewise be unfocused and without hierarchy, but in *Williams Mix* (1952), a tape collage that I personally take to be the principal neglected masterpiece of Cage's musical oeuvre. Here we find, in the scrupulously nonclimactic succession of very brief unconnected moments, a most thorough repudiation of classical ideas of form.

Oddly, it was in his visual art that Cage more rapidly realized his characteristic structure. Consider the drawing titled *Chess Piece* that Cage contributed to a 1944 exhibition of works related to Marcel Duchamp's interest in chess. It has a checkerboard pattern, at once reminiscent of both the chess field and the artistic constructivists with whom Cage initially had an affinity—remember that by 1944 he had already spent a year teaching at Moholy-Nagy's Institute of Design in Chicago. However, look closer and you will notice that no part of this work is more important than any other—the white does not predominate over the black, the center squares have no more emphasis than those on the outside. Moreover, not even the professional musician would know in which direction to read this collection of staves, because no square is intrinsically superior to any other; the array of squares has neither a definite beginning nor a definite end. A later visual work, descending from unintentional purposes and yet eminently Cagean in its artistic style, is the untitled drawing made by Cage while cleaning his pen during the composition of *34'46.776"* in 1954. The scattered ink lines create noncentered, nonhierarchical space, incidentally resembling, more than anything else, not painterly constructivism but expressionist paintings by Jackson Pollock, who, we remember, was likewise concerned with the possibilities of noncentered, nonhierarchical visual space.

Before returning to Cage's music, I want to look at certain scores from the 1950s, which are in a different way visually nonhierarchical and nonfocused. That is, where a conventional music score consists of horizontal staves that function to direct attention from left to right and from top to bottom, the Cagean score from this period is a field of visibly independent aggregates that can be played in any order; and further to eschew the possibility of a structural climax, the pages of *Winter Music* (1957), for instance, are unnumbered, which means that they can be played in any order. By such initially visual devices, Cage ensured that the aural experience of the entire piece will likewise be noncentered and nonclimactic.

Cage moved freely from art to art, nonetheless bringing his esthetic signature to new media and the new problems they pose. Of all the performance pieces he did, none was more spectacular, none was more exemplary of his radical esthetics, than *HPSCHD* as it was done at the University of Illinois at Urbana in May of 1969. While *HPSCHD* represents a great change from *Winter Music*—a change from spareness to abundance, from minimalism to maximalism—it still had the same Cagean structural devices conducive to the creation of noncentered, nonhierarchic, nonfocused time and space, full of activities that have neither a definite beginning nor a definite end. Indeed, the only feasible way to begin *HPSCHD* is to turn it on, as one might a switch, and the only way to conclude it, in this age of electricity, is simply to pull the plug.

Cage's later visual art is similarly unfocused and nonhierarchic; and here, as in his musical-theatrical works, Cage veered between visual fields that are very full—where the imagery fills the entire space—and visual fields that are very sparse. An example of the maximal is Cage's principal visual work of the late 1960s, *Not Wanting to Say Anything About Marcel*, done in memory of longtime friend Marcel Duchamp. For this Cage wrote remarks about Duchamp and then took them apart, distributing these verbal fragments on sheets of

Plexiglas that were then stacked one behind the other. There are few images other than letters and parts of letters. One strategy informing this work is that as you move from side to side, or come closer to it, the relationship between elements on each successive Plexiglas sheet changes, sometimes radically. Cage also derived a single lithograph from this work, and it too has the dense, all-over field reminiscent of Pollock. Cage's prints of the 1980s suggest the counterstrategy of spareness. Cage's veering between these two strategies of moreness and lessness reminds me of a generalization I have made often in the past two decades—that avant-garde art nowadays tends to have either much less stuff or much more stuff than art used to have.

John Cage was always writing; and in spite of his vehement objections to literariness, especially in the 1940s, he made consequential contributions to the experimental tradition of American writing. His first successful poetry, in my opinion, appeared in the *Diary* pieces of the late 1960s. The initial three diaries were reprinted in *A Year from Monday* (1967). It can be observed that they are a series of disconnected remarks, none more important than another, about a variety of subjects—art, reading, recent experiences, Cage's friends. Each remark is set in a different typeface, and the lines of poetry appear to break in an eccentric fashion. Cage explained this unusual design:

> The roman numerals identify the stanzas, the Arabic numbers the amount of words permitted to each typeface, the symbols refer to results derived from chance operations, as translated into terms suitable for consulting the *I Ching*.

Now that I have acknowledged Cage's use of the *I Ching*, I must confront his notorious interest in "chance." It has been my assumption, in over three decades of writing about Cage, that his use of chance is a minor issue and thus that critics of Cage who emphasize it, whether to praise or to blame, are missing the point. Chance is a method of composition—not a characteristic structure; chance is not perceptible—certainly not as perceptible as uninflected structure is, or the serial row is. Indeed, it is more useful to identify Cage's typical compositional strategy as fixing some parameters of a piece while allowing others to be left unspecific, which is to say left to chance.

For instance, in *HPSCHD* he requires that the fifty-one prerecorded tapes should consist of tones randomly produced within scales divided by every integer from five tones to an octave to fifty-six tones to an octave (except for the standard twelve tones to an octave). In brief, a computer is instructed to generate random tones within each of these fifty-one scales. However, once that requirement of fifty-one different divisions of the octave is established, it simply does not matter what sounds are laid on the individual tapes or in what order, or how loudly each tape is played at any point in the piece. The only possible result of playing all (or even half or some) of those tapes together could be microtonal din, which is precisely consonant with Cagean esthetics. As the result of purposeful purposelessness, not purposeless purposelessness, this is meticulously ordered disorder, which is quite different, in both construction and perception, from disordered disorder.

Similarly, once Cage ruled that a performance of *HPSCHD* would contain a large amount of slides drawn from many sources, in addition to an abundance of films and a wealth of screens, he determined many essential characteristics that would always be evident, regardless of particular details. Of course, chance methods are conducive to ensuring that the space and time within Cage's works will be nonhierarchic, nonfocused, etc.; but it is also possible that he (or anyone else) could realize such structural signatures without the use of chance methods. Indeed, Cage's discovery of his characteristic form preceded not only his involvement with that strain of oriental philosophy that encourages the acceptance of everything without connection and without discrimination, but his use of the *I Ching*.

In those books of his that he designed as well as authored, Cage likewise favored his signature form. I am thinking here not of *Silence*, where someone else had selected the work to be included, or even the later collections of his own fugitive writings, but of *Notations* (1969), which has always struck me as the quintessentially Cagean book. Here he published in alphabetical order sample pages of the works of several dozen contemporary composers. He invited the composers to choose their single-page contributions, rather than selecting them himself, because he felt he could trust them to represent themselves at their best. No contribution is billed as more important than any other; none is given more space than any other. This nonhierarchical structure represents a radical departure from the traditional notions of anthologies or magazines, which require that the editor "responsible for the book" put the best stuff toward the front and the weaker stuff toward the back; the responsible editor further indicates importance by featuring certain contributions on the magazine's cover or in the table of contents. *Notations*, by contrast, refuses the editorial options of focus and hierarchy. As Cage told an interviewer, his book "has this character of 'no value judgment,'" so that, he continued, "in one and the same collection there are good things and what people would say are poor things. And there are all kinds of things, and they're not organized into any categories. So that it's like those aquariums where all of the fish are in one big tank."

In his later poetry, Cage drew largely upon the language of others, first Henry David Thoreau and then James Joyce. For *Mureau*, the first of his Thoreau pieces, he extracted Henry David Thoreau's remarks about music and then reworked them by chance processes into continuous language that in certain qualities resembles prose more than poetry. Cage's later work with Thoreau, *Empty Words*, is more poetic, as Cage now used four classes of elements: phrases from Thoreau, words, syllables, and finally letters. In the four sections of the piece, the material becomes progressively more sparse. Nonetheless, *Empty Words* is, like its predecessor, finally nonhierarchical, nonfocused, uninflected, etc.

Cage extracted Joycean words from *Finnegans Wake* in a succession of inventive ways. It seems indicative to me that Cage should be drawn to the only work of major modern literature that is likewise scrupulously nonfocused and nonhierarchical, a work that characteristically ends with the direct suggestion to return to its beginning. It concludes, we remember, "a way a lone a last a loved a long the" and begins "riverrun, past Eve and Adam's, from swerve of shore to bend of bay, brings up by a commodius vicus."

To my taste, the richest of these Cagean workings with *Finnegans Wake* is *Roaratorio* (1979). Here the plan was to gather local sounds from all the geographic locations mentioned in the *Wake*; and since roughly half of the places are in Ireland, most of these location sounds are audibly Irish. More than two thousand separate acoustic elements were mixed on three sixteen-track machines and then four sixteen-tracks into an hour-long piece. Underneath this dense chaos you can hear, as a sort of ground bass comparable to the Mozart harpsichord music in *HPSCHD*, Cage himself reading from one of his reworkings of *Finnegans Wake*.

My interpretation of Cage has been reductionist, I admit; for while acknowledging his diversity, I have sought to identify his imaginative signature in a variety of artistic forms. The reductive suggestion is that Cage confronted each new medium with a definite set of artistic strategies. But this curt summary is not quite true. It is more accurate to say that whereas a monoartist attempts to invent variations on his personal style, the polyartist finds new media for his signature. The polyartist imposes a profoundly different interpretation upon the critical issue of consistency amid variousness—his unities are horizontal, across the arts, rather than vertically down into a single one.

II.

> The anarchist believes in a state of society where-
> in there is no frozen power structure, where all
> persons may make significant initiatory choices in
> regard to matters affecting their own lives.
>
> —Jackson Mac Low, "Statement" (1965)

With that image of anarchism in mind, we can see that there are political implications to Cagean structuring. Cage was interested in creating models of diffusion and freedom. That is what made him, in short, an anarchist libertarian. What makes Cage's art special, and to my senses politically original, is that his radical politics were expressed in decisions not of content but of form. For instance, one quality of *HPSCHD*, as well as many other works of his for large ensembles, is that they do not need a conductor. By extension, Cage was implying that outside of music, as well as in, it is possible to create social mechanisms that likewise can function without conductors—without chiefs. In other words, in the form of his art, in the form of performance, is a representation of an ideal polity.

It is precisely in relinquishing traditional opportunities for authority that Cage is making political decisions. As we know, his scores are designed to encourage variety of interpretation. There is no "right way" to do them, though there are wrong ways, especially if a performer violates instructions that are not left to chance. (In my opinion, the major problem for future Cage criticism will be comparative evaluating of performances.) A second reflection of his politics was writing music for an ensemble of equals, even when he was one of the performers, thereby resisting such conventional hierarchical forms as a soloist with a backup group. (The fact that this last feature was always true, except for a single piece from 1957 to 1958, indicates to me that Cage subscribed to his egalitarian politics long before he was conscious of them.) Thirdly, the principle of all notes being equal extends to objects, as all instruments are equal, regardless of their differing traditions. In *Credo in Us* (1942), for instance, the piano has no more presence than the home radio or phonograph; all should be equidistant from the audience. Fourth, Cage performed his music in gymnasiums as well as opera houses, the assumption being that all venues are equally legitimate. Fifth, his ideal universe was less a state than the preconditions for society. As Paul Goodman put it, "The libertarian is rather a millenarian than a utopian." In another context, Robert Nozick wrote, "Utopia is metautopia: the environment in which utopian experiments may be tried out; the environment which must, to a certain extent, be realized first if more particular utopian visions are to be realized stably."

One assumption of a compilation like *Notations*, with its equal portions of contributor-selected works in alphabetical order, is that the editor has no more authority than the reader in assigning value. The absence of hierarchy in this book likewise reflects his politics. Yet a traditional editor would huffily characterize a book like *Notations* as "an abdication of professional responsibility." Anyone who has ever worked in theater with Cage knows that he believed every performance venue should have convenient exits so that spectators can leave whenever they wish. Capturing anyone's attention, as we say, was to him no more justifiable in art than in life. One truth of Cage's own functioning was that no one loses anything by relinquishing power, and the essence of his method was not to tell but to show.

One thing that fascinates me about Cage was the purity of his anarchism. His perceptions were true to his politics; in neither his speech nor his behavior did I find the kinds of contradictions and conscious compromises that some political people think are opportune for ultimate ends. He was utterly free of pretenses to superior humanity or false snobbism. I've always regarded Cage as epitomizing the noncompetitive life, where no one is regarded as a threat who must be eliminated, where you can afford to be generous with your own work as well as your possessions, with art that is so extreme and idiosyncratic that plagiarism need not be feared. As he always made a point of publishing his writings in small magazines as well as large, it is not surprising that his 1980s piece on the Satie Society bypassed book publishing entirely to become available only on a modem-connected computer. Even his philosophy is true to his politics, at a time when, to paraphrase Barnett Newman, philosophy is for the artist, especially for some painters nowadays, much as the Bible is to the minister—which is to say a respectable source that can be used to justify anything. I have read scores of interviews with Cage and have never found him saying anything about his art that was demonstrably false.

Another thing I admire about Cage is that, especially in contrast to many post-socialists of his generation, he never doubled back. He never said that an earlier position of his was now unacceptably radical. As a result, he never was an ex-anything in either his esthetics or his politics. His art, as I noted before, has always displayed the anarchist characteristics I'm defining here. I would judge that one reason for his confidence late in life, in politics as well as esthetics, is that he knew from the beginning that he was never wrong, which I hasten to add is not the same thing as being always right, especially in politics.

I should also add that simply becoming a polyartist is itself a libertarian gesture, an assertion not only that the old pigeonholes should be exploded but that no one art has a necessarily higher status than any other. Need I say that given the professionalism of the arts in America now it is also a libertarian act to publish poetry without benefit of an M.F.A.—the literary license, so to speak—or to try to compose music without benefit of a D.M.A.

In my book *Conversing with Cage* (1988), which is a mosaic of passages from interviews he has given over the years, the concluding chapter is called "Social Philosophy." Here Cage is asked about having power: "I think we should go over our language and remove all words having to do with power. There are a number of composers who are interested in music becoming more political. They say that our social situation boils down to who has power and who doesn't. If that were so, I'd want to be one of those who were powerless." He continues, "I don't like the words 'greatest' or 'strength.' People are simply different from one another."

When he is asked, "Do you vote?" he answers, "I wouldn't dream of it. I'm looking forward to the time when no one votes. Because then we wouldn't have to have a president. We don't need a president. We can get along perfectly well without the government," which is the modern wisdom that the apolitical can be wiser, or less dangerous, than those who claim to be politically engaged.

Elsewhere Cage objected to the idea of total employment as a social goal: "What we need is a society based on the final possibility; finally we are able to have unemployment. Most people will tell you that this idea of loving unemployment is foolishness, because they are afraid that all those people who have nothing to do will go out and murder one another. This is simply like the bankruptcy of the city, the bankruptcy of the whole society; we don't have confidence in one another. Think of yourself and imagine whether you would murder other people if you had nothing else to do. You know perfectly well that you wouldn't. Why should we think so badly of other people?"

The last example is more subtle but profound in showing how his political bias led him to question a shibboleth of conventional philosophy. Bear in mind that Cage was participating in a symposium moderated by the biologist-philosopher C. H. Waddington. Someone else says, "I have a feeling that at present the world has lost a sense of unity at almost all scales, from the individual through these intermediate neighborhood groupings right up to the world scale." Cage replies, "I don't find the notion of unity . . . ," but he is cut off by his question-er: "I should not have said 'unity'; I should have said 'whole-ness.'" Cage continues: "Well, how was it that you should have said 'wholeness' and you did say 'unity'?" I have been thinking about this question of unity and multiplicity, and for myself I prefer multiplicity. It seems to me to conform more with our circumstances than unity does."

So the other guy replies: "Unity was a mistake; come on to wholeness." Cage continues: "But the mistake is very reveal-ing. Wholeness—the only objection I see to wholeness is that it suggests that there are boundaries to the whole, and then wholeness is like unity. I would rather have 'open-ness,' not unity or wholeness but open-ness—and open-ness particularly to things with which I am unfamiliar."

One Cagean tactic that always puzzled me in reading interviews with him is how he often rationalized an esthetic move in terms not of ideology but simply of social benefit. For example, he said of his *Freeman Etudes* for violin: "They are intentionally as difficult as I can make them, because I think we're now surrounded by very serious problems in the society, and we tend to think that the situation is hopeless and that it's just impossible to do something that will make everything turn out properly. So I think that this music, which is almost impos-sible [to play], gives an instance of the practicality of the impossible."

Once I recognized this tendency toward social rational-ization in Cage's commentary, I was skeptical about it, thinking it might have represented a certain opportunism. The more often I saw it, I came to recognize Cage as someone who matured in the 1930s, when ideas about social betterment through art were more prominent. Indeed, that ethos is the cen-ter of his polyartistry. To me, Cage is essentially a 1930s lefty, more interesting than others who came out of that period because he made some original perceptions not only about art but especially about the place of politics in art, and then the possible role of art for politics, all the while remaining true to the sentiment of that time. In my sense of Cage, Zen and chance and everything else came afterwards; they are merely icing on this anarchist cake.

Part II. The Works

• method • structure • intention • discipline • notation •

indeterminacy • interpenetration • imitation • devotion •
• **method** • **structure**
circumstances • method • structure • intention • discipline
• **intention** • **discipline**
notation • indeterminacy • interpenetration • imitation •

devotion • circumstances • method • structure • intention•
• **notation**

discipline • notation • indeterminacy • interpenetration • imita
• **indeterminacy**
• devotion • circumstances • method • structure • intention •

• **interpenetration**
discipline • notation • indeterminacy • interpenetration •

• **initiation**
imitation • devotion • circumstances • method • structur

• **devotion**
intention • discipline • notation • indeterminacy •

interpenetration • imitation • devotion • circumstances • me
• **circumstances**
• structure • intention• discipline • notation • indeterminacy

interpenetration • imitation • devotion • circumstances • me

• The Keystones of the Cagean Canon

The history of misunderstanding Cage's music is almost as long and as rich as the development of his compositional art. Very much aware from the beginning of those who were getting it wrong, I tried very hard to get his music right.

There is no question that John Cage ranked among the most prolific contemporary composers. His catalog (from C. F. Peters) lists over two hundred separate scores and it is hardly complete. However, looking back on the totality of his work, I find that some musical peaks are higher than others. Because Cage, like no other composer in history, had an importance and influence apart from the appreciation of his musical creations, and although he refused to discriminate evaluatively among his works, one feels obliged to identify the very best compositions—in my most severe judgment, *Europera* (1987), *Roaratorio* (1979), *HPSCHD* (1969), *Williams Mix* (1952), *The Sonatas and Interludes for Prepared Piano* (1946–1948), and no more than one other. (In several interviews, Cage himself said his best single work was *4'33"* [1952], his so-called silent piece; but those who concur are mostly his detractors!)

One quality that these Cagean masterpieces have in common is a grandness of conception—they take a single idea and explore it exhaustively, at length. As Cage said in another context, "What we want now is quantity; we get quality automatically." In *Europera* the idea is an inclusive pastiche of not just a few classic operas but the whole operatic tradition. *Roaratorio* is an acoustic "adaptation" of James Joyce's *Finnegans Wake* that is as Irish and yet as universal as the original. In *HPSCHD* the idea is the grandest mix of harpsichord music from Mozart to the present on one hand and scrupulously uninflected microtonal din on the other. In *Williams Mix* Cage used the newly developed technology of audiotape for a capability unprecedented in audio-storage media—it could be cut apart into hundreds of small fragments that were then reassembled into a continuous tape that, played at 15 ips realized an abundant rapidity of articulation impossible with live instruments.

• Early Piano Music (1935–1952)

*F*rom his musical beginnings, Cage regarded the piano as his primary musical instrument. Maturing out of a childhood ambition to devote himself to performing Edvard Grieg, he later earned much of his modest income by accompanying dancers. (Indeed, many of his early piano works were first composed for the dance pieces of his closest professional associate, the choreographer Merce Cunningham.) And so, too, the piano music written between 1935 and 1948 reflects Cage's general musical progress in the earliest period of his compositional career.

Two pieces composed in 1935, when Cage was twenty-three, used simple structures (which Cage calls "motives") that are subjected to a series of variations in two pianistic voices; for if the emphasis in Western music had long been on tonal relationships, Cage resolved instead to ignore his acknowledged incapacity and call attention to rhythm. Few early pieces were harmonically organized; following Schoenberg's dictum about the importance of all-determining form, Cage concentrated instead on structuring duration. *Metamorphosis* (1938) reveals a highly personal application of the serial principle, as both interval and rhythm are strictly fixed, though the row of tones is subject to the three standard serial manipulations of inversion, retrograde, and retrograde-inversion.

Cage's opening works displayed a taste for one of the great ideas of modern art: the use of imposed constraints to avoid old-fashioned habits, such as tonality and familiar rhythm. That is, the limiting rules function paradoxically to free Cage's compositional decisions from conventional patterns; nothing composed by serial procedures, for instance, could possibly sound like Grieg. Indeed, compositional constraints can include not only structural ideas, like serial procedures, but physical hazards, like Cage's most notorious device for deflecting habit, as well as perhaps his most famed invention: the prepared piano that was first used in *Bacchanale* (1938).

"The need to change the sound of the instrument," Cage later noted, "arose through the desire to make an accompaniment, without employing percussion instruments, suitable for the dance by Syvilla Fort for which it was composed." Cage at the time had been collecting an arsenal of percussion instruments, so that his doctoring of the piano, usually by inserting bolts or large wooden screws between the strings, connected one instrumental enthusiasm to another. Simply, his piano preparations transformed an instrument of limited timbre into a more acoustically various percussion "ensemble" under the control of a single player.

What seemed at the time a most radical innovation now takes its place in a respectable modern tradition that extends the rejection of traditional tonality into nonpitched sounds or "noise." Atonal music, we remember, admitted the full range of annotated tones, which numbered twelve between the octave scale. The next step, taken by a succession of twentieth-century composers, involved the use of sounds between those twelve tones. Charles Ives was among the first, in pieces composed for two pianos tuned a quarter tone apart; and Henry Cowell himself created severe pianistic dissonances, such as those made by depressing whole blocks of successive tones, that bore little resemblance to early twentieth-century "atonality." Perhaps Cage's most influential precursor was Edgard Varèse's *Ionisation* (1931), a totally percussive piece which employed such nonpitched sound generators as sirens and brake drums.

Cage's later pieces for the prepared piano extended these ideas, as he used in *The Perilous Night* (1944), *Root of an Unfocus* (1944), and *The Sonatas and Interludes for Prepared Piano* (1946–1948) not only bolts and wooden screws but also glass and rubber, all to distort considerably the pitch, duration, timbre, and envelope (degree of attack and decay) of the original piano sounds. While the scores for these pieces, as well as others composed at this time, contain conventional musical notations, Cage customarily attached some highly detailed illustrated instructions for doctoring the instrument for that particular piece. "These mutes produce a variety of timbres whose pitch and tone quality," Cowell wrote appreciatively at the time, "suggest the sound of gamelan or the jalatarange, with some delicate buzzes, clacks, hums, and sometimes an unaltered tone as well."

The piano piece *Tossed As It Is Untroubled* (1943) introduces a new rhythmic system based on numerical procedures for relating small parts to large parts; schemes of this kind were subsequently pursued in *Prelude for Meditation* (1944) and *Music for Marcel Duchamp* (1947), which was originally composed to accompany the Duchamp sequence of Hans Richter's avant-garde film *Dreams that Money Can Buy* (1948). Even radical art inevitably reveals precursors, and these pieces sound somewhat like the Polynesian music that Cage assimilated in Cowell's classes.

The composer-critic Virgil Thomson, writing in 1945, judged that all these inventions left Cage "free to develop the rhythmic element of composition, which is the weakest element in the Schoenbergian style, to a point of sophistication unmatched in the technique of any other living composer." Indeed, their distinctive rhythms and unusual tonalities make these pieces as instantly recognizable as Cage's own face and voice. The paradox is that although his compositional constraints largely function to deny both personal habit and tasteful choice, they also create a particular style of sound in time that is unmistakably Cagean. *Dreams* (1948), a piano piece originally composed for Cunningham, depends upon sustaining resonances for unusually long durations; and *Suite for Toy Piano* (1948) exploits the juvenile instrument's unusual timbre and the restricted range of tones—only the nine "white" keys from the E below middle C to the F above.

The historical irony is that pieces so radical at their origins now seem so obviously acceptable, if not charming, as well as a bit dated. The remarkable truth is that the avant-garde revolution initiated by Varèse and Cage has long since been won—witness both the dissonance and electronics used by rock groups. "How else can you explain a phenomenon like this," Cage observed in the late 1960s. "In 1933, '34, '35, somewhere along there, it took seventy-five rehearsals to put on Edgard Varèse's *Ionisation*. Right now, with students out of the Midwest at the University of Illinois, with two rehearsals we can get a better performance." And Cage himself, needless to say, pursued his earlier predilections for antitonal, antistructural sounds through a succession of aurally chaotic pieces, produced by unusual instrumental combinations ranging up to whole armies of electronic sound generators.

Nonetheless, he continued to exhibit a special affection for his primary instrument. His single most notorious composition (or anticomposition), the "silent piece" officially entitled *4'33"* (1952), was originally composed for piano; but since no intentional sounds are made, it could just as legitimately be performed on any other instrument(s). And one of Cage's later works, *Cheap Imitation* (1969), is intentionally an echo, produced by formulas deduced from *Socrate* by Erik Satie, who also favored the keyboard for his compositions. To John Cage's inventiveness, for the piano and everything else, after 1948, there was no end until his end.

• Sonatas and Interludes (1946–1948)

*T*he *Sonatas and Interludes for Prepared Piano* represents the culmination of Cage's work with the solo prepared piano, which had been his initial musical invention a decade before. Essentially, into the bed of piano strings he put a panoply of devices that transformed the sound of the piano strings.

What makes the work more significant than Cage's other prepared-piano pieces from that time is not only its greater length but its completeness. It is indicative that though many works for solo prepared piano came before the *Sonatas and Interludes*, only one, and it much shorter, followed it. (Two consequential successors, *34'46.776"* and *31'57.1499*, both from 1954, are for prepared piano in possible concert with other instruments.) The success of the *Sonatas and Interludes* partly accounts for why, in the following year, 1949, Cage received his first major awards: not only a Guggenheim Fellowship but a grant from the National Institute of Arts and Letters. It, more than anything else he had done to that time, showed his colleagues that Cage should be considered an important composer.

The score for this work has notes on staves—in the great tradition of compositions for piano—in addition to precise instructions about what to place on the piano and where. The performer should follow Cage's instructions exactly, or as exactly as possible, the foreign objects distorting timbre and envelope (degree of attack and decay) but *keeping the original pitches*. In other words, Cage retuned not pitch but other elements of piano-produced sound. Nonetheless, what all the sound-modifiers introduced into Cage's music was the possibility of indeterminacy, which is to say that the aural results included unexpected sounds that would not only never happen with unimpeded piano strings but could not happen again in subsequent performances. Only later did Cage provide graphic "scores" that were designed to encourage not just performers' flexibility but more radical preconditions for creating aural surprise.

One theme we can attribute in retrospect to Cage is the discovery of alternative acoustics for a row of keys, which makes his prepared piano a pioneering prelude to the electronic pianos that surround us today, with their expanding rhythmic and tonal range within a context (and keyboard) that echoes the classic instrument. (A similar contemporary paradox is that true dexterity at the personal computer depends upon the late nineteenth-century art of touch-typing!)

In the scope of ambition and the quality of individual moves, these *Sonatas and Interludes* also belong among other exhaustive modern masterpieces for the piano: Shostakovitch's *Preludes and Fugues* (1950–1951), Hindemith's *Ludus Tonalis* (1943), Messiaen's *Vingt regards sur l'enfant Jesus* (1944), and William Duckworth's *Time Curved Preludes* (1979). Listen to Cage's *Sonatas and Interludes* once and you will recognize that it holds its own in this most distinguished company.

The truth to remember is that Cage was first a pianist, which is how the musicians' union has always classified him; and to the extent that any individual instrument can be at the root of his compositional imagination, it is the piano. However, just as his *4'33"* was superseded a decade later by *0'00"* (1962), which is permission for any activity for any duration ("a solo to be performed in any way by anyone"), so Cage's later masterpieces were for other instruments.

About his *Sonatas and Interludes* Cage made two statements that have been reprinted before and, given their appropriateness, should be reprinted again (because they cannot be adequately paraphrased). The first deals with his sense of the piece's philosophical themes: "After reading the work of Ananda K. Coomaraswamy, I decided to attempt the expression in music of the 'permanent emotions' of [East] Indian traditions: the heroic, the erotic, the wondrous, the mirthful, sorrow, fear, anger, the odious and their common tendency toward tranquility."

In a 1964 C. F. Peters catalog of his compositions, Cage made these remarks about the work's structure: "The first eight, the twelfth, and the last four sonatas are written in AABB rhythmic structures of varying proportions, where the first two interludes have no structural repetitions. This difference is exchanged in the last two interludes and the sonatas nine through eleven which have respectively a prelude, interlude, and postlude." On the other hand, given nonclimactic, nonhierarchical structure that has always been typical of Cage's work, one gets the impression that the sections could indeed be played in a different order.

It has long been said that Cage is a composer not of talent but of genius, and that is not untrue. As his principal teacher, Arnold Schoenberg, told him that he had "no feeling for harmony," his subsequent career could be seen as representing a series of inspired strategies around, or compensations for, this inadequacy. Cage has also admitted that he has "no ear for music," which is to say his scores do not tell him exactly how his pieces will sound. Only in performance can he "hear" his work; the key to his experimental attitude is that he discovers by doing (or having it done). One reason why he worked so far outside the musical tradition was that those insufficiencies that might have discouraged a lesser imagination instead became the foundation of an alternative edifice. His example remains an inspiration to all of us handicapped artists.

• A Conversation About Early Works for Radio and Tape

In this 1985 conversation, a portion of a longer interview, Cage discussed with me the genesis of some of his early works for radio and audiotape, including the assembly of *Williams Mix* (1952).

When did you first work creatively with radio?
When I went to Seattle and took the job as dance accompanist for the classes of Bonnie Bird, I was attracted there in the first place by the presence of a large collection of percussion instruments; but when I got there I discovered that there was a radio station in connection with the school, like a big outhouse. The same building is still there, though now it's used, I think, for pottery. But then it was radio, and we were able to make experiments combining percussion instruments and small sounds that required amplification in the studio. We were able to broadcast those to the theater which was just a few steps away, and we were able, of course, to make recordings and, besides making records, to use records as instruments.

How did you use records as instruments?
Well, the record makes a sound and the speed of the record changes the pitch of it, and the turntables that we had then one no longer sees; but each one had a clutch—you could move from one speed to another.

What did you do in the radio station that you couldn't do playing the records live?
Well, the turntables were in the radio station, they were not movable, and they had speed controls. When you change the speed of the record, you change the frequency of the recorded

sound. I used continuous sounds that were made for test purposes by the Victor Company, and they had both constant
tones and tones that were constantly sliding in pitch through a
whole range. Those records were used in the *Imaginary Landscape No. 1* [1939].

Were the turntables played simultaneously?
No. That may have been the case somewhere in the piece, I forget; but they were played simultaneously with other instruments like cymbals, prepared piano, and so forth. Generally,
the record player would play one record at a time and then I'd
change it and play another record.

So you could go swiftly from one record to another.
Not swiftly, but you could go properly.

*Was the sound modified at all after it went into the micro-
phone?*
No, no, I've never done much with sound modification.

Why not?
I found the sounds interesting as they were.

*Let me ask about your experience of radio at that time.
What kind of radio did you listen to?*
I have no distinct recollection of ever listening to radio.

When you were young . . .
No, I do remember now. I can take it back a little bit. I had a
tendency to listen to the news.

Did you like radio comedy?
No. My mother and father did, but I didn't.
  There's one thing you probably don't remember, or do
you? When I was twelve years old, I had a radio program. It
was for the Boy Scouts of America. I rode on my bicycle from

Eagle Rock, where we lived, over to KFWB in Hollywood. I told them that I had the idea of having a Boy Scout program and that the performers on the program would be Boy Scouts and that ten minutes of each hour would be used by someone from either a synagogue or a church who would give some kind of an inspiring talk, you know. I was in the tenth grade, and so KFWB told me just to run along.

So I went to the next radio station—KNX. It was nearby, and they liked the idea, and they said, "Do you have permission from the Boy Scouts to do this?" I said, "No, but I can get that." So I went to the Boy Scouts and said that I had the agreement of KNX to have an hour every week for the Boy Scouts and was it all right with them? They said yes, and I said, "Well, will you cooperate with me? For instance, can I have the Boy Scout Band?" And they said, certainly not. They said you can do anything you like, but we won't cooperate; so I went back and told the people at the radio station. They agreed that every Friday after school—I was still in high school—I would go over to the radio station and conduct the program which I think was something like four to five in the afternoon or five to six. During the week I would prepare the program by getting as many other scouts as I could to play, oh say, violin solos or trombone solos.

If this was in 1924–1925, radio was still new to America.
Well, radio was very close to my experience, because my father was an inventor. He was never given the credit for it, but he had invented the first radio to be plugged into the electric light system.

What was your idea for the show?
Well, what I told you: Boy Scouts performing and some ten-minute inspirational talk from a member of the clergy. I no sooner began the program than there was a great deal of correspondence, people writing in; and those letters would be read

on the air by me. I was the master of ceremonies. When there was no one else to perform, I played piano solos, mostly *Music the Whole World Loves to Play*. There used to be these books with that title. They were on all the neighborhood pianos. It's sad that we no longer have pianos in every house, with several members of the family able to play, instead of listening to radio or watching television.

How long did your juvenile radio career go?
That lasted for two years. Isn't that amazing? And it was so popular that it became a two-hour program, and the Boy Scouts became jealous. They came to the radio station and said that I had no authority and no right to have the program. So, of necessity, the radio station asked me to leave, and they accepted the real Boy Scouts, because I was only second-class. I was not even a first-class scout. They accepted the real ones, and the real ones used it in a quite different way. They were very ostentatious and pushy. The result was that after two programs they were asked to leave.

Was there a sponsor?
No, this was before the day of grants.

Was the program aimed at other teenagers, or was it for an adult audience?
Well, the Scouts all loved it and so, for instance, did very elderly women, who were at home listening to the radio.

What other radio experiences do you remember from the twenties?
I was very impressed by the Columbia Workshop plays; *they* seemed to be worth listening to. My mood for entertainment, when I was young, was satisfied by such things or by those beautiful Russian films—Eisenstein. Mostly I felt above Hollywood, where I was more or less living.

Did you hear music on radio that interested you?
I don't remember hearing music. We'd go to the Hollywood Bowl for that.

So, even into the late twenties your experience of music came mostly from live music.
From piano lessons and so on. It was in church primarily. Aunt Marge had a beautiful contralto voice. I loved to hear her sing, always on Sundays in church and sometimes on weekdays at home. Then in college, at Pomona, I met a Japanese tennis player who had some kind of physical trouble as a result of playing tennis. So he was resting by taking a few classes at Pomona College. He was absolutely devoted to the string quartets of Beethoven, and he had as fine a collection of recordings of those as one could find. His name was Tamio Abe, and he played all those records for me.

The recording medium at that time was wire. Did you ever think of working creatively with wire?
I did some library research work in connection with my father's inventions. Because of that, when I became interested in recorded sound for musical purposes or even for radio plays, I then did library research for myself about the new technical possibilities; and they included, as you say, wire and film. Tape wasn't yet, in the early forties, recognized as a suitable musical means; but wire and film were.

Did you work with them yourself?
No, I just wanted to. I wrote letters, I think it was in '41 or '42, to corporations and universities all over the country trying to establish a Center for Experimental Music, and I didn't get anywhere. Well, actually, I got a little where. The University of Iowa's psychology department was interested through the presence there of, wasn't his name Carl Seashore, who made many ways of finding out about intelligence and so on. He was inter-

ested in my project. Dr. Aurelia Henry Reinhardt, isn't that right, who was president of Mills, was interested. She was a very tall, big, imposing, and brilliant woman. She had a great collection of Gertrude Stein books. So was Moholy-Nagy at the School of Design in Chicago. But none of these people had any money. They said, if I could raise the money to establish it, they would be willing to have it as part of their activities. For two years I kept trying to do that, and that's when I, so to speak, didn't get anywhere.

What did you imagine this center having?
Well, I was working with percussion instruments. One characteristic of percussion is that it's open to anything else than what it already has. The strings in the orchestra are not that way—they want to become more and more what they are; but the percussion wants to become other than what it is. And that's the part of the orchestra that's open, so to speak, to electronics. . . . And so I thought of recording means as instrumental to percussion music.

"Recording means"?
Records, films, tape, wires, anything; so that a center for experimental music would explore new possibilities for the production of sound.

Isn't that "sound modification"?
No, it could involve new instruments like the instruments of Luigi Russolo. My letter, which I wrote and sent to all these corporations and universities, always began with the history of experimental music in the twentieth century and that begins, I think, with the work of the Futurists in Italy.

But that's the history of new machines for music. . . .
Yes, new instruments; but, you see, machines are one thing and records are simply other kinds of machines.

You weren't interested in records for recording yourself as much as you wanted them as sound sources.
Right.

Because they had sounds that were not normally available to you?
Well, you can record any sound and then you can play any record and then you have an instrument.

Where did radio fit in this vision?
It had turntables.

Did these variable-speed machines we talked about before go from one predetermined speed to another, or did they have intermediate speeds?
They did; that was what was marvelous. You could go absolutely completely through the spectrum of possibilities from slow to fast. And it had clutches to go from one speed to another. The transition was not abrupt, but gradual, and produced amazingly interesting glissandi which you hear in my *Imaginary Landscape No. 1.*

What was your next radio involvement—the Kenneth Patchen project?
Yes, I always admired, as I told you, the Columbia Workshop play programs, and you remember the story of the play that had to do with the end of the world and how the entire country thought it was true; so that not only I, but many other people, were interested in the Columbia Workshop plays. I appealed to Davidson Taylor here in New York to let me make the accompaniment to a Columbia Workshop play. I explained to him that my view of radio music was that it should follow from a consideration of the possible environmental sounds of the play itself; so that, if it was a play that took place in the country, it would be natural to have the sound of birds and crickets and frogs and so forth. But, if it were a play that took place in the city, it would be

natural to have the sounds of traffic. In other words, I wanted to elevate the sound effect to the level of musical instruments.

That appealed to him and so he asked me to suggest an author for the play. The first one I suggested was Henry Miller. I asked Henry Miller if he would write a play for me, and he said it would be better if I would first read his books. It was difficult at that time to read his books because they were considered pornographic, so he gave me a letter of special introduction to the New York Public Library when I was still in Chicago. I came to the New York library where he said his books actually existed, and I was able to read them. I didn't see the possibility of a radio play from those books and still felt that he should write something especially for the occasion. He didn't agree to do that. So Davidson Taylor said, well, who would be your next choice, and I said Kenneth Patchen. I had read and enjoyed *The Journal of Albion Moonlight* [1941].

I was now living in Chicago, and I'd made friends with the head of the sound-effects department of CBS there. Since this was now a CBS Workshop project that had a particular date and deadline, I asked him what sounds I could use; and he said there's no limit to what you can do. (Musicians frequently say this to you also; they say, write anything you like and we will do it.) So I proceeded. I used to go downtown into the loop in Chicago and close my eyes and listen and I dreamed up through that listening all sorts of requests which I wrote down verbally and musically; and when I took them to the sound-effects man, he then told me, if you please, that what I'd written was impossible.

Just as those solicitous musicians would tell you that the score you'd just given them was impossible.
Right, so I said, what's impossible about it? He said it would be so expensive. By this time the projected performance was only a few days away and my whole score, which was for an hour, yes, of music that I had written, was, he said, impossible. I had to write another hour in just a few days, and I used the instruments

that I knew how to use—namely, the percussion instruments and records. The play that Kenneth Patchen had written was called *The City Wears a Slouch Hat* [1942]. I stayed up for about four days really without sleeping, just napping now and then; and I wrote. I was married then to Xenia Cage, and she would do the copying. We had the musicians on hand to play and so forth.

So they would play the new score as you were writing it down.
Essentially yes. I would write it, she would copy it, and they would play it.

Does that first score still exist?
No, I don't think so.

Can you reconstruct it? Could it be done, given technologies available now?
It might be able to be done, but I'm not going to do it.

Why were these early pieces called "Imaginary" Landscapes?
It's not a physical landscape. It's a term reserved for the new technologies. It's a landscape in the future. It's as though you used technology to take you off the ground and go like Alice through the looking glass.

Were your other, later Imaginary Landscapes likewise involved with radio?
They were involved with those turntables, but I didn't think of them as necessarily being involved with radio, but rather as being necessarily involved with new technological possibilities.

That were available in radio stations.
Or elsewhere, so that if I found something in a moving-picture studio, for instance, like a film phonograph, that would have been suitable material for an Imaginary Landscape. Later, the

Imaginary Landscape No. 4 [1951] was for twelve radios, and *No. 5* [1952] was for magnetic tape.

How did you develop the notion of using radio as a musical instrument?
There was a tendency through the whole twentieth century, from the Futurists on, to use noises, anything that produced sound, as a musical instrument. It wasn't really a leap on my part; it was, rather, simply opening my ears to what was in the air.

Do you remember your thinking at that time?
Yes, my thinking was that I didn't like the radio and that I would be able to like it if I used it in my work. That's the same kind of thinking that we ascribe to the cave dwellers in their drawings of the frightening animals on the walls—that through making the pictures of them that they would come to terms with them. I did that later with the tape machine in Milan when I went to make *Fontana Mix* [1958]. I was alarmed over all the possibilities, so I simply sat down the first day I was there and drew a picture of the whole machine.

That dehexed it for you, so to speak.
Right. It's true.

Now why did you choose twelve radios, rather than just one, for Imaginary Landscape No. 4?
There are so many possible answers; I don't remember which one was in my head. One is the twelve tones of the octave, and the other is the twelve disciples, and so on. It seemed like a reasonable number.

It's said in the history books that when you saw them lined up, you said, "Ah, twelve Golden Throats." Now I assume that's ironic.
No. This particular radio I was using was advertised as a "Golden Throat."

But did you think of them as "golden throats"?
Yes, because, when I was walking along one of the streets in the Fifties near Radio City and these radios were in the window, they were advertised as "Golden Throats," and I immediately decided to go to the president of the company, or the manager of the store, and ask for the loan of twelve of them. I did that, and he gave me the loan.

So, with your exclamation of "twelve Golden Throats," you basically gave him free advertising.
Exactly.

Didn't you have two operators for each radio?
Right. One controls kilocycles and the other controls the tone control and the volume.

And what instructions did you give the performers?
The parts were written in what we call proportional notation, where the notes are at the points in space that they should be in time. However, this is written in a space which changes with accelerandos and ritards; so that it's at the cross between conventional notation and proportional notation. The *Music of Changes* [1951] is at the same point, so it's written in 2/2 or 4/4. The space is observed, so that fractions of notes that are irrational can be placed in it by measuring them. Then I can go, for instance, from a note that's two-fifths of a quarter to a note that's one-third of a half, and so on, and measure each single fragment. In this case, because you're measuring, you need not add up to whole units; you can come out completely uneven.

Which is not so easy to do in straight musical notation.
No, but I was still using quarter notes and half notes, and half notes you see with fractions above them, very peculiar. Later, due to David Tudor's studying a form of mathematics, to take the trouble out of my notation and doing it successfully, I

dropped all notion of meter and went directly into plain space-equals-time, which has enormously facilitated the writing of new music.

Were those twenty-four radio performers musicians?
Yes, they were. They could all read notes, and there was a conductor who was beating 4/4 time.

Who was he?
I was doing it.

My recollection is that there was something special about what time of day this performance was.
The first performance had almost no sound in it. Two friends of mine at the time, Henry Cowell and Virgil Thomson, both attributed the absence of sound to the fact that it was late at night—it was nearly midnight. However, I knew that the piece was essentially quiet through the use of chance operations and that there was very little sound in it, even in broad daylight, so to speak, because the volume levels would always be very low.

Tell me about your other works for radio at that time.
Radio Music [1956] and Speech [1955] "for five radio and newsreader," it says in your catalog.
Well they're slightly different, but the radio piece was written more or less to please the people who were disturbed over the *Imaginary Landscape No. 4* because it was so quiet. I forgot what I did, but it can be played so as to be loud.

Your catalog of twenty years ago says that in Radio Music *"durations of tunings are free, but each is to be expressed by maximum amplitude."*
It does. Well then it's obvious that that's what it was. If people wanted radios to be loud, that was the piece to play.

Is it basically the same piece?
No, it's relatively indeterminate. It has a different score. I haven't looked at it recently; it's really not very interesting.

How did your writing these pieces change your attitude to radio, at least in your personal life?
It made it possible for me to listen to radio with great interest, no matter what it was doing.

And what did you listen to then?
Well, anything that I happened to hear. I didn't myself turn on a radio to listen to it; but when I was going through the streets or when a neighbor was playing the radio and so forth, I listened as though I were listening to a musical instrument.

Did radio become a favorite musical instrument?
Almost as favored by me as the sounds of traffic.

When you were driving the Cunningham troupe around the country in the fifties, did you have a radio in the bus?
No, we played Scrabble.

When did you first encounter audiotape?
I must have first encountered it in Paris in the late forties, when I met Pierre Schaeffer, who was the first to do any serious work from a musical point of view in relation to magnetic tape. He made every effort he could to get me interested in working along those lines, but I wasn't yet really ready. I was writing my *String Quartet* [1950], and I had written *Sonatas and Interludes* [1946–1948]. I was gradually moving towards the shift from music as structure to music as process and to the use, as a result, of chance operations in composition. I might have been more cooperative with Schaeffer, but I wasn't. It didn't really dawn on me.

Because of notational problems?
No, my mind was being used in a different way; so that I

wasn't as open as I might have been to the notion of music on magnetic tape then. That's '49.

In '52, when I worked with David Tudor and Earle Brown, we made several pieces—one by Earle, one by me, one by Christian Wolff and one by Morton Feldman, with funding from Paul Williams. I made the *Williams Mix* then. All of that work was done with excitement over the possibilities of magnetic tape, and they were various. That's why I was anxious not to exploit them alone but with other people, because each mind would bring into the new possibilities a different slant; and that's certainly the case. Feldman was working with his early graph music, and it was just marvelous to come to a square on his graph paper with the number, say, 1,097 in it. That meant that we were to chop up a piece of recorded tape so that it formed 1,097 fragments and splice it back into the band, you know, at that point. I was very open at the time, and very interested in splicing tape and in making the music manually. I found various ways of changing sound not with dials but, rather, by physically cutting the tape.

Such as?
Well, the tape normally goes past the head horizontally; but if you cut it and splice it back diagonally, . . .

You would have to cut it into such small pieces that, in effect, are no longer than tape is normally wide.
Yes, but you could get perfectly beautiful sounds by putting it at an angle to what it should have been.

That's terribly meticulous work.
Yes, and I was using chance operations, so that I was able to go from a vertical cut on the tape to one that was four inches long at an angle on quarter-inch tape.

It must have taken years.
Well, no, it took about a year with help to splice the *Williams*

Mix, which was itself a little over four minutes of music; but we did other pieces. We did the *Suite by Chance* of Christian Wolff, and we did the *Octet* of Earle Brown, and we did the *Intersection* of Morton Feldman. Earle's piece was made with the rubbish from the pieces by Feldman and Wolff and myself.

Using similar compositional operations?
Using his own composing means, but with regard to the sounds that were, so to speak, thrown away through the process of making other pieces.

You know that I regard the Williams Mix *as your most neglected masterpiece.*
Well, it's an interesting piece. One reason it could very well be neglected is that the score has nearly five hundred pages and, therefore, it has not been reproduced. The original is at [C. F.] Peters, I think. It would be too expensive to multiply it; so I don't think many people are aware of it. I have illustrated it in the notes to the Town Hall program.

The twenty-fifth anniversary album.
People have seen one page that is like a dressmaker's pattern— it literally shows where the tape shall be cut, and you lay the tape on the score itself.

On the scale of one to one?
One to one, yes.

So the tape is, in effect, the length of five hundred pages.
Yes, each page has twenty inches, two ten-inch systems, a little over a second in duration.

Which are, in the album illustration, reproduced on a single page, one atop the other. Your idea for this score is that it would be possible to reproduce the cuts with tapes other than what you used.

Yes. I labeled each entry in the score according to the categories which were A, B, C, D, E and F and hoped with those categories to cover all possible environmental sounds. Then I took the various parameters of sound as little letters to follow those capital letters of the categories. So that you would know what kinds of transformations of those original environmental sounds had been made, whether the frequency had been changed or the loudness had been changed and so forth; so if it was the same as it was originally, it was followed by a "c." If it had been varied, it was followed by a "v." So "Accv" would be a sound, let us say, from the country that had remained as it was in two respects and had been changed in a third.

And this "Accv" you would have gotten by chance operations.
Right. And then you could have a sound described as "Avvc" or "Bcvc" or their combination "AvvcBcvc," and someone else then could follow that recipe, so to speak, with other sources that I had to make another mix. It really is very interesting, don't you think?

Fantastic, yes. As you say, the score is like a dressmaker's pattern. You just simply lay it out and duplicate its cuts on your tape.
One of the pages has a hole in it, which came from a burn from a cigarette. I was a great smoker in those days.

To me, two of the special qualities of the Williams Mix *are its unprecedented range of sounds and the rapidity of their articulation.*
Right. What was so fascinating about tape possibility was that a second, which we had always thought was a relatively short space of time, became fifteen inches. It became something quite long that could be cut up. Morty Feldman, as I told you, took a quarter of an inch and asked us to put 1,097 sounds in it, and we did it—we actually did it.

Within a quarter inch?
Which would be one-sixtieth of a second, you see—we put 1,097 fragments.

Without mixing? You mean just little slivers of tape?
Little slivers of tape.

That's physically impossible.
No, no, we did it.

How?
By counting, and by hand.

You were crazy.
Oh, of course, it's crazy; but then don't you think it's true of both of us that we've been crazy all along?

Speak for yourself. I'm not that crazy.
Norman O. Brown told me once that any worthwhile activity is mad. And the only reason it ever is taken seriously eventually is that one persists.

But, as you pointed out, even though you made for posterity a score of Williams Mix *for others to realize, no one's ever done it.*
But it's because the manuscript is so big and so little known.

What was your next involvement with tape?
Imaginary Landscape No. 5 was for tape, and it was simply made for a dance by Jean Erdman. It was called *Portrait of a Lady* [1952], and the dance had a kind of character that suggested popular music. So I wrote a score that would make use of records—jazz records in this case, but they could be records of other kinds of music—treated as sound sources, rather than being what they were.

How long were those segments?
They were very short too.

*Did you destroy any reference to their original sources? Was
this collection as various as that for* Williams Mix?
I don't recall whether I made the choice or whether Jean Erdman made the choice or whether it was made by the two of us;
it must have had something to do with chance operations.

Does that tape still exist?
The score exists, and Jean probably has the tape. I don't myself
know where it is.

*What else did you do with radio between then and the late
seventies?*
One might consider the piece *Works of Calder* [1951], the recording
or composition I made for it. I first went to the studio of Calder with
the idea of recording sounds of the mobiles bumping into one another; this would be a proper accompaniment for a film about his work.
I had two ideas in mind. One was that and the other was to write
a piece of music, such as my *Sonatas and Interludes* or *A Valentine
Out of Season* [1944] or *The Perilous Night* [1944] or something
that would accompany the film that was made by Herbert Matter.

When you say something like that you mean . . .
A musical, so to speak—a more conventional musical.

*But also something of some length—that would be elaborate
within itself.*
And that would take the structure of the film into consideration.
    I mean the story isn't being properly told because the
piece for twelve radios actually comes after the *Works of
Calder*, but *Works of Calder* includes the attitude that I had
toward the sound being appropriate to the story or film, and
that's why I wanted the sounds of the studio. What happened

in the end was that the *Works of Calder* has both the sounds of the studio in one section and that it has, before and after that, more conventional musical accompaniment ideas.

The sounds of Calder's studio relate back to your idea of the sounds for the Patchen piece.
Yes. Since this film was about the mobiles of Calder, to go into his studio and tape the sounds of mobiles bumping into one another as the proper accompaniment for such a film.

And again to take those sounds straight—not to modify them in any way.
Right.

When did you first discover multitracking?
What do you mean, "multitracking"?

Multitrack tape.
But my idea all along was to have each track be individual, so that the relation of the tracks could be independent of one another, rather than fixed in a particular scorelike situation.

But that wasn't possible with the Williams Mix *because in those days you had only monophonic tape.*
Well, it was, because we made the *Williams Mix* for eight separate mono tracks.

Eight separate mono tracks, to be played simultaneously?
Right, and they can't be fixed together, you see, in a particular way, though they are fixed that way for practical purposes, for Peters' publishing them, for instance; but you can rent the single tracks, or tracks in pairs, or in fours.

You mean to say that the Williams Mix *I hear on that twenty-fifth anniversary record . . .*
Is a performance of eight separate tracks.

Eight mono tracks, played simultaneously within a period of roughly five minutes.
Four minutes and twenty seconds, something like that, or fifteen.

And you're saying that all eight of those tapes are autonomous elements of the piece.
They're parts, and there is a score—that dressmaker's score; but it isn't possible to get it precisely together.

A score for playing all eight tapes at once.
Well, to make them, to splice them, and theoretically, of course, they would all sound together; but the synchronization of eight things is not possible. That's why multitrack came into existence, sixteen-track machines and so forth; but I consistently refused to use it.

Why?
Because that would give *one* fixed relation to separate tracks.

So, therefore, the version on that record is not definitive.
I've all along spoken against records at the same time that I've permitted their being made and have even encouraged it; but I've always said that a record is not faithful to the nature of music.

Which can only exist in a live performance situation.
Right, right, right. I've always been a proper member of the musicians' union, in favor of live music.

And what is your instrument of virtuosity?
I'm listed in the union as a pianist.

I'm still going to ask you when you first used multitrack.
Every time that I've used it, I've been careful not to use it. Also that is to say all the individual parts can be separated from the congregation—the score of all of them together in one way. That's true of *HPSCHD* [1969], which has something like fifty-six parts.

Fifty-six monophonic parts?
Right, and it's true of *Roaratorio* [1979]. How many parts does it have?

Over two thousand?
No, that's the number of sounds of something, but the number of parts is different.

How do you measure parts in Roaratorio?
Well, the number of individual tapes that could be used to make up the total. I don't think we've ever had a performance with more than, say, twenty-eight machines, whereas we had a performance of *HPSCHD* with fifty-six machines.

In Urbana, Illinois, where there weren't any multitracks either. What you've done, in effect, is made pseudomultitracks. No, that's not quite the right word either. You've made choruses of autonomous monophonic tapes that cannot be synchronized.
Right.

In effect imitating the condition of the multitrack technology without taking advantage of its unique capability to organize everything.
Yes, I haven't wanted to fix the relationship of individual parts. And that continues and is in my present writing for instrumental music for the recent *Thirty Pieces for String Quartet* [1983], and with the *Music For* [1984], which is for anywhere from one player to, I think, eight now, where there's no score but there are all these parts that can got together in a variety of unpredictable ways.

• Indeterminacy (1959)

For most of the world, most of the time, John Cage was an international avant-garde composer; for me he has always been an innovative American writer. My introduction to his writing came not from something in print but from *Indeterminacy*, which appeared as a two-record box a few years before his first book, *Silence* (1961). Until then, you would have had to see Cage perform to appreciate his more imaginative writing; very little of it had ever appeared in print.

The idea behind *Indeterminacy* was, like many Cagean ideas, essentially simple if audaciously original. In one acoustic space he would declaim any of ninety very short stories, taking a minute to finish each one. Thus, those with many words were necessarily read quickly; those with a few words, slowly. In another room, beyond earshot of Cage, the pianist David Tudor, by that time a veteran Cage collaborator, was playing miscellaneous sections from his parts for Cage's *Concert for Piano and Orchestra* (1957–1958), occasionally playing as well prerecorded tape from another Cage composition, *Fontana Mix* (1958). As Cage wrote at the time, "David Tudor was free to make any continuity of his choice. There was no rehearsal beforehand involving both the reading and the music, for in all my recent music there are parts but no score."

Cage's stories tend to fall into several groups. Some are meant to be illustrations of his Buddhist devotion to his esthetics of accepting all sounds as equally legitimate. At a respite following a Zen service, he remembered, "The hostess and her husband, employing an out-of-tune piano and a cracked voice, gave a wretched performance of an excerpt from a third-rate Italian opera. I was embarrassed and glanced toward the Roshi to see how he was taking it. The expression on his face was absolutely beatific." Before a demonstration like this, Cage was forced to learn how far he had to go.

A recurring theme is overcoming adversity, as Cage tells the story of his teacher Arnold Schoenberg informing him that he had no feeling for harmony. "He then said that I would always encounter an obstacle, that it would be as though I came to a wall through which I could not pass. I said, 'In that case I will devote my life to beating my head against that wall.'" What happened, of course, is that Cage made a constraint of his defect, composing a music so consistently devoid of harmony that it was scarcely missed.

Some stories here portray Cage's love for nature and especially of mushrooms. From them follow stories of his cooking and eating not just mushrooms but cabbages and hot peanuts. Yet others tell of the experience of touring, not only as a solo musician but as the music director of the Merce Cunningham Dance Company. He liked to recall the witty remarks of his friends, such as the painter Jasper Johns and the late composer Morton Feldman. Few, to my recollection, speak of his reading, or his experience of art, or his opinions about music. Some are funny in the tradition of Mark Twain—an eternally innocent writer surprised at the foibles of the world. Like traditional comedy, but unlike tragedy, Cage's stories assume that all will turn out well in the end.

The acoustic innovation is the one-minute story, declaimed at speeds reflective of the stories' lengths, in sum redeeming the otherwise decadent form of the solo literary recital. *Indeterminacy* also represents Cage's comment on poetry and jazz, a complementary mixing of music and language that was popular in the 1950s. Always there is an elegance and wit that are uniquely Cagean, for even in print his stories display a distinctive prose. Since he was always the most adept performer of his own writing, *Indeterminacy* gives the unusual stories an even more unique voice. He later used these texts, along with new ones composed within the same constraint, as his contribution to the Merce Cunningham choreography, *How To Pass, Kick, Fall, and Run* (1965), the dancers replacing

David Tudor, so to speak. The paragraph-long story was a form, a constraint, that Cage mastered, much as he would later master the mesostic.

The texts for many of these stories may be found in Cage's first two books, *A Year from Monday* (1967) and *Silence*. In the latter they appear not only in the chapter marked "Indeterminacy" but scattered throughout its pages, "playing the function that odd bits of information play at the ends of columns in a small-town newspaper," as Cage put it. He continues: "I suggest that they be read in the manner and in the situations that one reads newspapers—even the metropolitan ones—when one does so purposelessly: that is, jumping here and there and responding at the same time to environmental events and sounds." It follows that the disc *Indeterminacy* need not be heard in silence; it is perfectly appropriate to play it in a space filled with other sounds, even the noise of traffic, or radios that could be playing yakety-yak as well as music.

One key to Cage's esthetic is the absence of hierarchy. Just as no story in *Indeterminacy* is necessarily more important than any other, so none is necessarily a beginning of the piece and none necessarily an end; they resemble slips of paper that are picked at random from a bowl until the bowl is empty. "My intention in putting the stories together in an unplanned way," Cage writes in *Silence*, "was to suggest that all things—stories, incidental sounds from the environment, and, by extension, beings—*are* related, and that this complexity is more evident when it is not oversimplified by an idea of relationship in one person's mind." It follows that the listener should feel free to reorder the sections of the compact disc into as many sequences as he or she wishes, for the new disc technology grants listeners permission to become interpreters in assembling the various parts.

For the performances of Cage and Tudor there were no definite beginnings and no definite ends. Quite simply they began apart from each other and played until time ran out. Since each performer had his own stopwatch, there was reason to expect they would end around the same time. *Indeterminacy* exemplifies the flat, uninflected structure of superficially disconnected events that has always characterized Cage's music and, to no surprise, Merce Cunningham's dance. This scrupulous absence of hierarchy reflects not only Zen Buddhism, which Cage studied intensively at Columbia University in the late 1940s, but an anarchism that has informed his art and activities since the 1930s.

One theme is that indeterminacy differs from improvisation because indeterminacy incorporates imaginative constraints. The idea of the poetry-jazz duets was that speaker and musicians would respond to one another, each spontaneously trying to reinforce the other, customarily in habitual ways. The principle of indeterminacy allows each performer to work apart from the other, indeed in this case unaware of each other, each with scores designed to minimize habit. If a reader is required to speak only fifteen words in sixty seconds, he or she cannot resort to pet ways of phrasing.

Those familiar with avant-garde contemporary radio, especially as it is produced in Germany, can identify *Indeterminacy* as early *Neue Hörspiel* in that it is primarily an innovative acoustic experience, involving speech as well as sounds. Indeed, *Indeterminacy* could be characterized as a radio program (that wouldn't benefit from a picture) of an avant-garde kind that wasn't produced in America at that time. It could also be classified as an early Cage "play" in a distinguished theatrical career.

Though Cage was to my mind a major American prose writer, you won't find his name in any history of American literature, nor will you find any articles about his writing in the annual indicies of the *Publications of the Modern Languages Association*. Even in this age of extensive study of contemporary literature, of the National Endowments for the Arts and the Humanities, it is still possible for a well-known American writer to do distinctive work that, notwithstanding his fame as a composer-esthetician, is academically ignored.

• A Year from Monday (1967)

A *Year from Monday*, Cage's second collection of fugitive pieces, is rich in ideas relevant to all sorts of artistic, philosophical, and social endeavors. Cage was so emancipated from professional conventions that he could freely follow his imagination into any medium and risk innovative work in areas other than music. Though his ideas invite disagreement, even from the sophisticated, I doubt if any open-minded and intelligent person would not be challenged—surely irritated, perhaps persuaded to change his mind—in the course of perusing this compendium of provocative aphorisms, intellectual flights, and formulations so original they will doubtlessly make sense to some, nonsense to others. However, just as Cage could not write a linear expository essay (and his book itself cannot be "read" in the conventionally linear way), so I find myself unable to compose a traditionally structured critical piece about him. *A Year from Monday* is so fertile and various that one must dip in, pick out, and think about whatever strikes the mind, and that process itself informs the structure of these miscellaneous paragraphs. A further truth is that writing about Cage brings out, for better and worse, one's courage for waywardness.

One must initially acknowledge Cage's indisputable originality in an age that suspects everything has already been done; for nearly all that he made, whether in art or life, was riddled by idiosyncratic and imaginative touches. He talked like no one else, conducted his personal existence like no one else, composed performance pieces like no one else, and, as this book amply demonstrates, wrote as no one else would dare. (Even its original price, $7.92, represents a minor innovation, which was perhaps part of a one-man quixotic campaign to induce 1 percent as an appropriate sales tax.) He took even his most comic ideas very seriously and asks us to do so too—and to laugh as well. His penchant for the unusual gives his writing the quality of constant surprise; for this reason much of it is not immediately comprehensible, though his thought is not particularly complex. Even at the beginnings of his artistic career, Cage managed to be ahead of the herds; and, as he continued to forge new frontiers, even the most aggressive younger bulls grazed art-historically behind their esthetic daddy.

With this book, the author of a revolution in music clearly wanted to accomplish something similar for exposition; and although the desired breakthrough still seemed a few steps away, Cage was by now discernibly beyond literary conventions: "My pleasure in composition, renounced as it has been in the field of music, continues in the field of writing words; and that explains why, recently, I write so much." In his earlier collection of pieces, *Silence* (1961), the later essays eschewed linear organization for the structure of random comments. In this book few collections of sentences are even as approximately linear as this paragraph. The discontinuous compositional style seems an appropriate vehicle for Cage's invariably unconventional thoughts as well as an approximate literary analogy for his scrupulously discontinuous music; yet precisely because the style continually risks unfamiliarity, it signifies that Cage was still more of an artist than a propagandist.

One radical artistic idea that Cage pushed beyond its previous provinces is the work of art as primarily an esthetic illustration. The illustrative point of *4'33"* (1952) is that all the unintentional, random sounds framed within that auditorium and within that period of time can be considered music. "Doing nothing," as the critic Jill Johnston put it, is clearly "distinct from expressing nothing." By investing a situation where sophisticated contemporary music is expected with nothing intentionally audible, Cage implied that in the silence was "music" that could be heard. This polemical illustration exemplifies the principle of "art by subtraction" to the point that negation produces addition—in Mies van der Rohe's felicitous phrase, "Less is more."

Because Cage invariably took the intellectual leaps his radical ideas implied, he subsequently concluded that not only were any and all sounds music, but that the time-space frame of four minutes and thirty-three seconds was needlessly arbitrary, for unintentional music is indeed with us—available to ears that wish to perceive it—in all spaces and at all times. (*Variations III* [1964], he once told me over dinner, is so open, "We could be performing it right now, if we decided to do so." Another time he mentioned juvenile pieces composed by mathematical rules that "I destroyed because they didn't sound musical to me then, though I would probably think differently now.") From this, too, would inevitably follow another thesis, which holds that just as one does not naturally discern why one period of "silence" is better than another but rather perceives personal significances in chaotic experience, so it is likewise irrelevant to evaluate one conglomeration of noise against another. What matters, quite simply, is what the perspicacious ear manages to apprehend if not appreciate. "Value judgments are destructive to our proper business, which is curiosity and awareness," he often said. "How are you going to use this situation if you are there? This is the big question."

However, Cage also realized that, rather than deduce himself out of a career, he as an artist could program sound-generating instruments to produce an aural experience as random and miscellaneous as the unintentional noise on the street. So most of his performance pieces since the mid-1950s were unstructured, indeterminate, multifarious events. It is customary to call these works "chance" music; but since chance per se is not perceptible, I prefer to characterize them as musically chaotic. As artistic wholes these compositions differ from life in expressing a heightened incoherence, an appropriate scale, an absence of visual and aural focus—in short, an ordered disorder. Most are also not only flat in structure but thoroughly devoid of climax, development, emphasis, pacing, contours, and variations. Therefore, their components need merely be turned on until turned off by a formally irrelevant decision (for example: no more pages left in the score; the audience has completely departed; it's midnight; and so on).

The root of Cage's compositional principles was collage—the mixing of materials not normally heard together; but because he was less interested in barbed juxtaposition than abundant mixtures, the result is less collage than something distinctly Cagean. That roughly explains why an experienced ear, though it may not have heard a particular piece or rendition before, can usually identify a certain unfamiliar piece as Cage's work and not someone else's. In *Theatre Piece* (1960) he pursued an implication of *Music Walk* (1958) by suggesting, first, that a plethora of physical actions could, by a performer's choices, be substituted for randomly activated sound-generating procedures; and, second, that since he had previously ruled that all sounds are music, this instruction eventually implied, by analogy, that "theater" could be said to exist as soon as the perceiver's mind wished to define it. "Theater takes place all the time, wherever one is," Cage wrote in *Silence*, "and art simply facilitates persuading one this is the case." Nonetheless, it is precisely in their realized inchoateness and, in Cage's phrase, "purposeful purposelessness," as well as extravagantly spectacular qualities, that his own theater pieces distinguish themselves from both ordinary life (merely the "model" for the art) and "happenings" theater produced by others.

In retrospect, then, the primary significance of 4'33" lies precisely in its inferences, which gave Cage and others "reason" or permission to create eventually a musical theater that is indeterminate not only in its composition but its performance too—aleatory kinetic presentational structures that are chaotic in both structure and detail. What is most conspicuously lacking in *A Year from Monday* is an analogous path-finding gesture that could command as much suggestive influence for literature as his earlier "musical" demonstrations. Regrettably, Cage did not particularly develop his stunningly suggestive assertion in *Silence*: "I have nothing to say and I am saying it and that is poetry." That void was left for others to fill.

Adopting the musical notion of unashamedly artificial constraints to literary purposes, Cage posited unprecedented ground rules that served to emancipate him from conventional ways of organizing and rendering words. An instance of this, *Indeterminacy* (1959), consists of ninety very short stories, each of which is less than a minute in length when read aloud. When Cage performs this piece on a record of that title, while David Tudor makes random noises in another room, *Indeterminacy* is very much about variations in prose tempo as well as the random interactions between musical sounds and verbalized words. Here the form of the work expresses part of its ultimate content, as a performance illustrates (as opposed to explains) the piece's declarative title and Cage's esthetic position; therefore, the ninety funny stories, which are pleasurable in themselves and comic to various degrees, are just the surface occasion for less obvious but more substantial concerns. Here, as in much else of Cage's, the imperceptive spectator can be deceived into accepting the surface as the entire point—as silence is simply no sound, so stories are just anecdotes—but more significant meanings are invariably implied or inferred, by the piece, the spectator, or both. However, to put these stories into conventional print, as Cage does in *Silence*, destroys much of their primary effect (corrupting their original purpose even more than recordings of Cage's recent pieces betray, as fixed renditions, their scored indeterminacy). In the traditions of strictly printed literature, ninety funny anecdotes within a larger frame constitute no innovation at all. Similarly, another performance piece, "Juilliard Lecture" (1952), published in this new book, is in its printed form all but unreadable, as is "Talk I" (1965), which, as Cage's headnote reveals, was not intended to be understood anyway.

The major piece in *A Year from Monday* is a three-part "Diary: How to Improve the World (You Will Only Make

Matters Worse)," its sections subtitled respectively with the years 1965, 1966, and 1967. In composing what he characterizes as a "mosaic of ideas, statements, words and stories," Cage posited a system of compositional constraints and indeterminate procedures (which also constrain his expression) described in his headnote:

> For each day, I determined by chance operations how many parts of the mosaic I would write and how many words there would be in each. . . . I used an IBM Selectric typewriter to print my text. I used twelve different type-faces, letting chance operations determine which face would be used for which statement. So, too, the left marginations [sic] were determined, the right marginations being the result of not hyphenating words and at the same time keeping the number of characters per line forty-three or less.

In practice, these constraining procedures induce an original style with its own distinct tone and particular rhythms. The pieces of the "Diary" are "poetry," not because they manipulate poetic conventions but simply because they cannot be persuasively classified as anything else. However, as a form suitable primarily for miscellaneous insights and connections, prejudices and gossip (usually to an excess), anecdotes and speculations, it is also a rather needlessly limited vehicle for verbal expression. Although it enables Cage to note unusual analogies, to make one-line suggestions, to relate one kind of position to another, and to provide reviewers with numerous quotable gag lines (which are not representative of the text as a whole), this note-making format discourages the elaboration and development of thoughts and grants Cage an easy escape from the necessity (or opportunity) of pursuing the implications of his more radical ideas. On the other hand, precisely in its disconnectedness such prose demands that the reader make her or his own connections.

Beyond that, the form here, unlike that in *Indeterminacy*, suggests no conceptual content that I can perceive or infer (even though previous experience with both Cage and other avant-garde materials persuades me to add that I may well be missing the significance); therefore, the primary substance of these "Diary" pieces lies not in the form but the quality of the commentary, which is inevitably erratic, instinctively radical, and often stimulating. Finally, as a literary form appropriate for random remarks, this compositional process represents a successful mating of man and his makings; nothing could be more suitable, if not congenial, to an artist on the move—a man of (artistic) action, so to speak, as Cage was most of the time—as distinguished from a contemplative thinker or a professional writer. Perhaps because Cage derived an expression appropriate in form to his personal style, *A Year from Monday* is a more readable, communicative, and artistically suggestive book than its predecessor.

A major theme of *A Year from Monday* is fortuitous happenstance, as the book is riddled with observations on how delightfully random both art and life can be. Cage's definition of environmental reality arose from his esthetic bias: "We open our eyes and ears seeing life each day excellent as it is. This realization no longer needs art, though without art it would have been difficult (yoga, zazen, etc.) to come by." The theme of happenstance is implied in the book's title, whose spirit and significance the writer Jill Johnston has accurately explained:

> [It] refers to a projected rendezvous, with friends in Mexico, but who could say what would happen a year from Monday, much less a year from Tuesday, another day of interrupted designs; and so of course nobody went to Mexico, but one day Cage and Merce Cunningham bumped into Bucky Fuller in an airport outside of Madrid, which has nothing to do with the title of the book, or everything from the viewpoint of unpredictability in an ambiguous reference to time.

Another way to elaborate the theme might be: whatever someone plans for a year from Monday is not likely to happen, although something else will, which may be just as valuable, providing that the perceiver keeps his channels open to experience. "Only the unusual exists," runs a proverb from 'Pataphysics, "and everything is unpredictable, especially the predictable." However, given the style of discourse established by Cage's philosophy and the book's title, it seems nothing but inappropriate that its pages should be chronologically numbered and then snugly bound, or that this hardbound edition is beyond the budgets of most avant-garde readers, or that purchasers do not need to cut open the pages (perhaps to their own designs) to read them, or that the lectures and essays and such are reprinted in more or less chronological order (as if to demonstrate some fictitious development [!] in Cage's thought), or that a tape of Cage's inimitable voice is not included; but perhaps another implicit theme is that the conventions of familiar media inevitably compromise the furthest-reaching esthetics.

Most of the prose pieces collected in *A Year from Monday* deal with varieties of coherence in intentionally unstructured (orderly disordered) prose; and, even though Cage is more imaginative than most authors, including many of those who consider themselves "avant-garde," he neglects all the leaps his bias suggests. First of all, his headnotes to each essay are written in expository grammar; but, even though these notes are doubtlessly intended to make more comprehensible the material that follows, their conventionally linear form seriously compromises the revolutions in printed communications that the essays themselves imply. Second, even though each "Diary," for instance, uses an engaging variety of typefaces (thanks to IBM ingenuity), all the print is approximately of the same height; this is another limitation in the expressive possibilities of printed words. (All the print is black, which is another limiting convention, although the Something Else Press issued the third diary in a two-color edition, and the S.M.S.

Press published the fourth, dated 1968 and not collected into *Monday*, in three colors.) Third, in all the essays, not only is the type laid out in horizontal lines, but Cage also usually composes in sentences that, though often clipped short, similarly impose unnecessary restraints. Indeed, even though he must have known that precisely in syntax and linearity is the inherent conservatism of language as an expressive medium, Cage still strove for aphorisms, which are, after all, linear bon mots. Nonetheless, *A Year from Monday* represents a clear stylistic progression beyond the prose in *Silence*; for if an implicit motif of the earlier book was his quest for a literary style that would both express his thoughts and illustrate his esthetic ideas, Cage so patently forged to the frontier in this second book.

In the history of contemporary art, Cage functions as an antithetical catalyst who leaps ahead so that others may move forward by steps. Late in the 1930s he suggested prophetically that all noises, including those electronically produced, would enter the domain of serious music; by his use of sounds unfamiliar to concert halls he helped establish precedents for all contemporary electronic composition. Indeed, by making art out of materials not usually familiar to art, Cage, along with his mentor Marcel Duchamp, also provided antithetical precedents for pop art, found objects, industrial sculpture, and much else. Allan Kaprow, a sometime painter who originated (and christened) that performance art known as happenings, testifies that, although he personally does not subscribe to all of Cage's radical innovations, "he taught us to be free." In this respect, another implicit theme of *A Year from Monday* is that all kinds of criticism and all kinds of fiction, including critical fictions and fictitious criticism, can be put on pages, intermixed, and bound between hard covers.

Cage's impact upon artists working in the musical traditions can be perceived in all aleatory composition—the works of Morton Feldman, Christian Wolff, Earle Brown, David Behrman, early La Monte Young, and many other Americans, in addition to such major European musicians as Pierre Boulez and Karlheinz Stockhausen. However, whereas all these composers adopt aleatory techniques in various ways, only Cage holds to the extreme position that regards all sounds available to the ear as music (or all movements as theater). Still, no one dares imitate Cage's pieces, not only because they are in some dimensions so extreme, but also because, in the world of art, a certain kind of performance event is generally known as Cage's domain. ("Others could do them," he once confessed, "but they won't.") Instead, his radical antitheses have stimulated others to produce their own syntheses.

Sometimes Cage created radical antitheses for himself to synthesize—by acting in an extreme way, perhaps with a special kind of irony, an artist can force himself to entertain new thoughts. The fact that Cage formally presented *4'33"* scarcely a few times persuades me to believe that he knew, first, that this piece incorporates an ironic gesture, and, second, that he sometimes took positions finally unacceptable to sensible human beings, a category that includes himself. For instance, the first performance of *4'33"* theoretically granted him permission to explore the fullest range of sounds, both intentional and nonintentional, yet even though *4'33"* was in a fundamental sense artless, most of these subsequent works represent a synthesis. That is, they draw if not depend upon the posited antithesis as well as, of course, Cage's disciplined cleverness and his mastery of aleatory mixed-means dramaturgy. Similarly, although he deduced, as a radical antithesis to conventional practice, that he could not, in principle, offer critical opinions on art or life, the synthesis is that in fact he was a very opinionated, if not dogmatic, propagandist for his idiosyncratic taste and radical esthetic positions. In *A Year from Monday*, nonetheless, there are no discernible antithetical leaps; thus, no new syntheses are likely to follow.

Critics and laymen are forever debating Cage's place in contemporary music, and part of his originality lay in continually defying the categories by which we talk and classify, if not demonstrating, by his practice, how inherently philistine might be the boundaries themselves. Historically speaking, Cage descended from several distinctly modern musical traditions. One was concerned with introducing sounds previously unknown to formal music (for example, Edgard Varèse's *Ionisation* [1931]); a second emphasized the possible expressiveness of the theatrical space in which music was performed (for example, Charles Ives's *The Unanswered Question* [1908]); a third consistently eschewed classical tonality and structure, not for a new musical language with its own grammars of coherence, such as Schoenberg's twelve-tone system, but for more chaotic kinds of aural experiences. As a developing composer, Cage posited a succession of groundbreaking stylistic positions by logical—rather, paralogical—deduction. His first discrete style was percussion music that scrupulously avoided familiar pitches and rhythms (e.g., *First Construction [in Metal]* [1939]), and then he invented the prepared piano, which systematically perverted, in a minimally random way, the instrument's natural sounds for unusual aural effects. Particularly in the recorded *Sonatas and Interludes* (1946–1948), however, Cage's pieces for his home-brewed invention suspiciously echo the piano music of Erik Satie that Cage has publicly praised, confirming the esthetic principle that even avant-garde art comes out of discernibly previous art.

By the late 1940s Cage introduced aleatory techniques into the process of setting marks to paper, thereby abandoning premeditated control not only over the finished score but also, in some pieces, over how the score would eventually be performed. So far, Cage clearly had remained within musical traditions, having pursued a more or less straight path from premeditated scores and fixed performance to chance composition and indeterminate performance. The turnabout year was 1952, when he, first, composed *Williams Mix*, a tape collage, which, I find, represents his most valuable purely aural endeavor; second, presented the premiere of *4'33"*; and, third, staged an untitled mixed-means event at Black Mountain College in North Carolina that in retrospect seems to have been the first "happening" in America.

From here on, everything Cage did was, by his subsequent logical deduction, as much indeterminate theater as indeterminate music: *Radio Music* (1956) "for one to eight performers, each at one radio"; *Music for Amplified Toy Pianos* (1960); *Rozart Mix* (1965) for twelve tape machines, several performers, one conductor, and eighty-eight loops of audiotape; *Variations V* (1965), with Merce Cunningham and his dance company, films by Stan VanDerBeek, and a sensitized electronic field; the supremely spectacular theatrical environment *HPSCHD* (1969); and so on. His "scores" for these pieces, though published by a music company, offer not a precise plan for articulating sound but descriptive (often prose) instructions for generating activities that, like a football play, are likely to run out of intentional control—that produce "indeterminate" results. "I never imagine anything until I experience it," Cage once declared; but this is completely contrary to one of the basic tasks of musical training, solfège, which teaches one to examine a score and then imagine, or hear in one's head, the finished work. In *A Year from Monday* he defines his current art as a "process set in motion by a group of people," a kind of activity that, in the history of human endeavor seems closer to noncompetitive games than esthetic artifacts.

Rather than, as some antagonists would have it, abandoning inept musical composition for "stunts," Cage became the true master of mixed-means musical theater, perhaps the most valid American species of "opera"; it could be reviewed by the music critic or the dance critic, by the theater critic, the art critic, or, more usually, by none of them. To my sensibility these later pieces are far more interesting and valid as theater of mixed means than as purely aural art; compared solely as music with Milton Babbitt's or Elliott Carter's compositions, they seem feeble indeed. For that reason, not only are records of certain Cage works, such as *Variations IV* invariably embarrassing, but, in confronting a live experience of these pieces, one quickly discovers that purely musical values and categories do not provide satisfactory and/or relevant perceptual expectations or critical standards. (Also, if only to accept his pervasive Americanness, Cage ought to use the native spelling—"thea*ter*"—rather than, as he does, the European.) Indeed, in the history of theatrical events, Cage artistically descended not from literary drama but from such American exemplars as vaudeville, *Hellzapoppin'*, the Marx Brothers, Ives's unfinished Universe Symphony, and the dance performances of Merce Cunningham.

Partly because of Cage's immense influence, there now exist in each of the nonliterary arts in America two avant-garde tendencies, both of which are clearly distant from nineteenth-century conventions and discernibly different from pre-1945 practice. One would isolate the intrinsic qualities of an art—serial music, minimal and optical painting, early Merce Cunningham; the second would, like Cage, miscegenate—mix in enough materials, esthetic preoccupations, and structural standards from the other arts to ensure that something between, or *intermedia*, is created. Almost by definition, all miscegenated art ridicules the pigeonholes of both current critical enterprise and the academic departmental system, as well as the parochial esthetic values indigenous to each art; and, perhaps until periodicals recognize that they ought to sponsor critics of mixed-means work, artists such as Cage are less likely to be widely understood, let alone appreciated. On the other hand, there is some sense, as well as some irony, in Cage's radical suggestion that "now we have such a marvelous loss of boundaries that your criticism of a happening could be a piece of music or a scientific experiment or a trip to Japan or a trip to your local shopping market." Anything can be considered art; anything, theater; anything, criticism. Although his commitment to Zen persuaded him to oppose Western ideas of syllogistic logic, Cage consistently deduced an antithetical catalyst.

The news in *A Year from Monday* is that Cage has renounced music for social philosophy; but, just as he abandoned concert music for a mixed-means theater that subsumes his music, so he regarded his music, which has always been about changing people's minds, as a springboard into political thought. In retrospect we can see how much politics has always been present in his music. First of all, his music implies the abolition of archaic structures, as does his politics; and both his music and his social thought suggest that new forms ought to be built from the most essential materials:

> In music, it was hopeless to think in terms of the old structure (tonality), to do things following old methods (counterpoint, harmony), to use the old materials (orchestral instruments). We started from scratch: sound, silence, time, activity. In society, no amount of doctoring up economics/politics will help. Begin again, assuming abundance, unemployment, a field situation, multiplicity, unpredictability, immediacy, the possibility of participation.

In contrast to most modern artists, who have been pessimistic about both technology and the future, Cage, perhaps because of his "sunny disposition," always took the optimistic side; and his social prophecies indicatively parallel his artistic predilections. Just as Cage's performance pieces shrewdly exploit various electronic media in autonomous ways, all to create a field of intentionally nonstructured activity, so Cage insisted that technology can socially be considered more of a blessing than a curse. (His art is, after all, more appropriate for an age of television and take-home videotape than radio and phonograph records.)

In Cage's coherent web of related radical ideas, the major common theme is that, since great changes are still possible in both life and art, we should strive to achieve what has not already been done. Cage, in his social thought, concurred with good liberal prejudices: equality of opportunity, universal civil rights, equitable distribution of economic affluence, the elimination of discrimination and segregation, and so on; but, recognizing that liberal prejudice is not enough, he took, as usual, several leaps ahead. As an instinctive anarchist, he favored less work rather than more, or more unemployment rather than less, as well as a guaranteed annual wage to provide for those for whom no jobs exist. "Taxation could be augmented," he once remarked in passing, "to the point where no one had any money at all." Similarly, he expressed the anarchist's negative reaction to comprehensively detailed planning, noting of Le Corbusier (and, implicitly, of much modern architecture), "Art this is called. Its shape is tyranny." (Yet, he refused to acknowledge the totalitarian tendencies in Buckminster Fuller's thought.)

For situations of too much order, such as programmatic architecture and organizational bureaucracy, he championed disorder; for situations of needless disorder he supported overall ordering, such as centrally organized and universally free public utilities. He is enough of a McLuhanite to believe that a truly global electric voltage, as well as a universal design for plugs and jacks, could have a profoundly ecumenical effect: "Alteration of global society through electronics so the world will go round by means of united intelligence rather than by means of divisive intelligence (politics, economics)." Because automated technology promises more abundant leisure, if not the possibility of endless environmental pleasure and the obsolescence of most social and esthetic hierarchies, Cage wanted to install a psychology that would allow every man to appreciate constantly the "art" around him all the time; thus do the pedagogic purposes of his musical theater link to his optimistic visions for the future. I suspect that the final vision of his ecumenical anarchism would have all of us listening to everyone's 0′00″ together.

Although his bias was "not fixing [society] but changing it so it works," what *A Year from Monday* does not offer is a practical politics—specific advice on how the golden age will come—perhaps because Cage believed that widespread mind-change precedes social change. He sensed, not untenably, that technological development itself will initiate most of the trans-formations. "Once we give our attention to the practice of not-being-governed, we notice that it is increasing." This sense that the world is getting better largely on its own momentum may strike some political people as slightly naive; but Cage's profes-sional life exemplified its own kind of radical activism. As a man who frequently commanded audiences, spreading a cer-tain gospel, reprogramming the heads of those who learn to appreciate his "music," offering images and proposals for a radically different future, exercising his almost Jesuitical per-suasiveness—all at a time when most self-styled "radicals" offered merely negative criticisms—Cage was a harbinger-pub-licist for a new, necessary, comprehensive, unprecedented, unstructured, mixed-means revolution.

• HPSCHD (1969): Environmental Abundance

*F*lashing on the outside underwalls of the huge double-saucer Assembly Hall at the University of Illinois' Urbana campus were an endless number of slides from fifty-two projectors. Inside, between 7:00 P.M. and just after midnight on Friday evening, May 16, 1969, was a presentation of the John Cage–Lejaren Hiller collaboration *HPSCHD* (1969), one of the great artistic environments of the decade. In the middle of the circular sports arena were suspended several parallel sheets of visquine, each one hundred by forty feet, and from both sides were projected films and slides whose collaged imagery passed through several sheets. Running around a circular ceiling rim was a continuous 340-foot screen; from a hidden point inside were projected slides with imagery as various as outer-space scenes, pages of Mozart music, computer instructions, and nonrepresentational blotches. Beams of light were shrewdly aimed across the interior roof, visually rearticulating the modulated concrete supports. In several upper locations were spinning mirrored balls reflecting dots of light in all directions—a device reminiscent of a discotheque or a planetarium—and the lights shining directly down upon the asphalt floor also changed color from time to time. There was such an incredible abundance of things to see that the eye could scarcely focus on anything in particular; no reporter could possibly write everything down.

The scene was bathed in a sea of sounds that had no distinct relation to one another, an atonal and astructural chaos so continually in flux that one could hear nothing more specific than a few seconds of repetition. Fading in and out through the mix were snatches of harpsichord music that sounded more like Mozart than anything else. This music apparently came from the seven instrumentalists visible on platforms raised above the floor in the center of the Assembly Hall. Around these islands of stability were flowing several thousand people, most of them students at the university, some of whom came from far away: museum directors from Chicago and Minneapolis; writers, artists, and a film crew (doing a profile of Cage) from New York City; students who hitchhiked from all over the Midwest; and the not-young lady harpsichordist who first commissioned *HPSCHD*, all the way from Switzerland.

Most of the audience milled about the floor while hundreds took seats in the bleachers. All over Assembly Hall were people, some of them supine, their eyes closed, grooving on the multiple stereophony. A few people at times broke into dance, creating a show within a show that simply added more to the mix. Some painted their faces with Day-Glo colors, while, off on the side, several students had a process for implanting on a white shirt a red picture of Beethoven wearing a sweatshirt emblazoned with John Cage's smiling face. As in the Central Park be-ins, I met friends from various places I had not seen in ages, and other people I knew before only by mail.

While cocomposer Hiller checked on the machinery and its upkeep, though it scarcely mattered artistically if a few channels were lost, John Cage glided around the hall, beaming beatifically. Altogether, the sound was rather mellow and non-climactic, except for occasional blasts of eardrum-piercing feedback that became more frequent toward the end. Just after midnight, the electronic sound machinery was turned off, the mix ran down into silence, the house lights turned on, and the elated audience drifted out. At parties that night and the following day, people compared perceptions; while everyone saw the same things in general, each person registered specific experiences particularly his or her own.

The sounds came from fifty-eight amplified channels, each with its own loudspeaker high in the auditorium. Fifty-one channels contained computer-generated music composed in octaves divided at every integer between five and fifty-six tones to the octave (five tones, six, seven, eight, up to fifty-six, except number twelve). As all these channels were going at once, with each operator of the four assembled tape recorders permitted to adjust their respective volumes, the result was a supremely microtonal chaos in which, as Cage's Illinois colleague Ben Johnston put it, "It was ensured that no order can be perceived."

On top of this mix one could hear seven amplified harpsichords, for *HPSCHD* is that word reduced to the six characters necessary for computer transmission. Three were playing fixed versions of Mozart's late-eighteenth-century *Introduction to the Composition of Waltzes by Means of Dice*, in which the performer is allowed to play sections in any order she or he wishes. With computer assistance, Cage and Hiller realized three different fixed versions of the fragments, two of which incorporated other passages from Mozart. Two more harpsichordists, Neely Bruce and Yuji Takahashi, played through differing but individually fixed collages of harpsichord music from Mozart to the present, while David Tudor played a "computer printout for twelve-tone gamut." The seventh keyboard operator, Philip Corner, had nothing more specific than blanket permission to play any Mozart he wished; and every instrumentalist received this further instruction: "In addition to playing his own solo, each harpsichordist is free to play any of the others."

In sum, then, above the microtonal din were references to Mozart, a favorite classic composer of both Cage and Hiller. "With Bach," Cage explained, "there is a tendency to fixity and unity; in Mozart, there is scalar diversity and abundance. I used to think of five as the most things we could perceive at once; but the way things are going recently, it may be in a sense of quantity, rather than quality, that we have our hope. When you use the word 'chaos,' it means there is no chaos, because everything is equally related—there is an extremely complex interpenetration of an unknowable number of centers." For all its diffusion, therefore, *HPSCHD* is an indubitably organic piece, where every element contributes its bit to the whole and which successfully establishes a unique and coherent ensemble of interrelated parts.

So, the aural content of the work—what one should hear—is literally fifty-eight channels of sound, even though most of us can scarcely separate more than one or two from the others at any time. "You don't have to choose, really, but, so to speak, experience it," Cage added, between puffs on his filtered and mentholated cigarette. "As you go from one point of the hall to another, the experience changes; and here, too, each man determines what he hears. The situation relates to individuals differently, because attention isn't focused in one direction. Freedom of movement, you see, is basic to both this art and this society. With all those parts and no conductor, you can see that even this populous a society can function without a conductor." Cage characterized *HPSCHD* as a political art, which is not about politics but political itself: "As an anarchist, I aim to get rid of politics. I would prefer to drop the question of power, whether black power, flower power, or student power. Only by looking out the back window, as McLuhan says, do we concern ourselves with power. If we look forward, we see cooperation and things being made possible, to make the world work so any kind of living can take place."

The visual material was compiled under the supervision of Ronald Nameth and Calvin Sumsion, both connected with the university, and Robert Frerck supervised the use of films. There was no dress rehearsal, nor did the piece really need one. Forty-eight people, in sum, contributed to the performance. In the course of gathering equipment, Cage persuaded an awed official of the GAF Corporation to lend eighty Sawyer projectors ("He wanted not a few but eighty!"), just as he earlier persuaded other companies to lend fifty-two tape recorders and all the amplification machinery; and art students were enlisted to paint innumerable slides. NASA lent forty films and five thousand slides (accounting for the abundance of outer-space imagery), and the Museum of Modern Art extended a print of Georges Méliès's *Trip to the Moon* (1902). And so on and so on, all to fill up Assembly Hall with an indeterminate assembling of images, all to complement the indeterminate chaos of sounds.

Work on *HPSCHD* (pronounced "Hip-see-kid," "H-P-S-C-H-D," or, as Cage preferred, just "Harpsichord") began nearly two years before, just after Cage arrived at Illinois as Visiting Research Professor in the School of Music and Associate of the Center for Advanced Study. On hand he already had a standing commission from the Swiss harpsichordist Antoinette Vischer. Wanting to "make with the computer an art that has not been possible before," he sought out Lejaren Hiller, who pioneered computer-assisted composition. Together they produced the fifty-two tapes, many of which were composed with the *I Ching* using the randomizing procedures Cage had long favored. "Every single note was a mutual decision," Hiller declared. "It's a rather unique instance that two composers' endeavors are so intertwined that you cannot tell them apart." Nonetheless, the total conception of *HPSCHD* seems more distinctly Cage's than Hiller's, whose reputation stems from the use of computers rather than a distinct style; and, within the extant repertoire of electronic music, Hiller's tapes sound rather simple and repetitious.

Cage's regular music publisher, C. F. Peters, published a several-hundred-page "score," with seven different harpsichord parts; "a particular condensation of the piece," as Hiller puts it, was released by Nonesuch Records. Although only three of the harpsichord parts are included, the record offers a more intensified (and, shall we say, artful) aural chaos than the diffuse original; but that perhaps is precisely what a recording should do. Each album also includes a computer-printed instruction that, to quote Hiller, "tells the listener how to turn the volume and tone controls every five seconds to hear the piece properly. Every sheet is different, so you can trade it off like baseball cards." Although strictly aural recording is not an appropriate medium for such aleatory and spatial art, this remains, in my opinion, the best (and most) Cagean record ever made.

HPSCHD was not just a musical light show or an extravagant multimedia display but a masterful example of that peculiarly contemporary art, the kinetic environment, or an artistically activated enclosed space. In this respect, *HPSCHD* extends Cage's continuing interest in filling huge spaces with a lifelike chaos of sounds and sights, or building an artful universe within the larger world. Here, as before, Cage preferred nontheatrical spaces, like a gymnasium or a "stock pavilion" (scene of a 1967 Urbana piece), for his multiringed, highly theatrical artistic circus. Who would believe, before Cage arrived, that Urbana's Assembly Hall itself could be transformed into a work of art? Whereas *Variations VII*, by all accounts the best piece at the 1966 Theater and Engineering Festival, filled up the cavernous 69th Regiment Armory, *HPSCHD* tackled an even larger space, for an even larger audience, and made it succumb to his environmental art.

HPSCHD is a Universe Symphony in the distinctly American tradition dating back to Charles Ives, who spent the last forty years of his life on a similarly all-inclusive but unfinished work. As Ives imagined his Universe Symphony, groups of musicians would be distributed around the countryside—up the hills and in the valleys—and they would sound a joyful disorder similar to the last movement of his *Fourth Symphony* (1910–1916). However, thanks to technological progress, Cage and Hiller could use facilities Ives never had—tape recorders, amplifiers, loudspeakers, motion-picture and slide projectors—to distribute their chaotic art all over an enormous space; and in the increased quantity was a particular kind of quality never before experienced in either art or life. In the future, let *HPSCHD* turn on even larger spaces, like Madison Square Garden, the Houston Astrodome, or even the Buckminster Fuller dome that someday ought to be constructed over midtown Manhattan. Wish you were, or could be, there.

• Not Wanting to Say Anything About Marcel (1969)

> A mind that is interested in changing . . . is interested precisely in the things that are at extremes. I'm certainly like that. Unless we go to extremes, we won't get anywhere.
>
> —John Cage

Living most of his adult life in lower Manhattan, Cage befriended visual artists who were attracted by his commitment to esthetic freedom—to unfettered choice of materials in unrestricted combinations. Hardly anyone else was preaching such artistic principles in the 1950s. So, in retrospect, it is not surprising that he strongly influenced painters such as Robert Rauschenberg and Jasper Johns, both of whom became his personal friends, in addition to countless passing acquaintances and even strangers. The common opinion holds that no other individual has had as much influence upon advanced visual art, initially in America but also abroad, as Cage.

It could be said that of the arts in which Cage excelled, he was slowest to come to visual art. An early example is his *Chess Pieces*, done around 1944 for the Julian Levy exhibition of works related to Marcel Duchamp's interest in chess. (The only reproduction known to me appears in my documentary monograph, *John Cage* [1970, 1991].) What we see is a square chess-checkerboard in which half of the sixty-four squares have bars of musical notes in black while those squares adjacent to them have notes in white, all against a continuous gray background. Because there is no notational continuity from square to square in any direction, or even from one black square to the next black square (likewise in any direction), Cage is suggesting that the boxes can be read (or played) in any order—from top to bottom, or the reverse; from inside out or outside in or whatever. That is another way of saying that *Chess Pieces* has noncentered activity that is evenly distributed "all over," to the very edges of the work.

Another early work is an untitled drawing that Cage made in 1954 while cleaning his pen during a certain music composition. (It, too, is reproduced in *John Cage.*) Rescued at the time by his colleague the composer Earle Brown, this piece of unintentional art resembles a Jackson Pollock, who was likewise concerned with all-over nonhierarchical distribution; the drawing additionally looks forward to the cross-hatching that Jasper Johns introduced in the 1970s. Finally, the visual arts world was always predisposed to appreciate the exquisite calligraphy of Cage's musical scores, many of which were exhibited at the Stable Gallery in New York in 1958. As Dore Ashton wrote in *The New York Times* at the time, "Each page has a calligraphic beauty quite apart from its function as a musical composition."

In 1969, the year after Marcel Duchamp's death at seventy-nine, Cage was a composer-in-residence at the University of Cincinnati. Alice Weston, a local art patron, "got the idea that though I had not done any lithographs, I could do some. Marcel had just died, and I had been asked by one of the magazines here to do something for Marcel. I had just before heard Jap [Jasper Johns] say, 'I don't want to say anything about Marcel,' because they had asked him to say something about Marcel in the magazine too. So I called them, both the Plexigrams and the lithographs, *Not Wanting to Say Anything About Marcel*, quoting Jap without saying so."

Not wanting to say anything particular with language, Cage decided to use chance operations to discover words in the dictionary. At the time he was favoring the use of three coins that when flipped could yield Head-Head-Tail, HHH, HTT, THT, HTH, THH, TTH, TTT—eight different combinations.

So he made squares with sixty-four options (eight-by-eight), flipping one sequence of three coins to get the vertical location of a chance-derived square and then another sequence to get its horizontal location; therefore, any collection of possible artistic choices had to be divided into sixty-four alternatives. Taking the 1,428 pages of *The American Dictionary* (1955), Cage defined 20 groups of 23 pages apiece and 44 groups of 22 pages apiece. Once the coin flips forced him to isolate one group of pages, he flipped the coins again to find out which page. After counting the number of entries on that page, he did another set of flips to locate an individual word. Because some of these words had different forms (plural, past tense, gerund), he often flipped again to find out which one to use. Then he had other charts dividing 1,041 typefaces available in a standard catalog of press-on (Letraset) type. Once this was determined, he flipped again to discover whether to use uppercase letters or lowercase. And then another time to discover where in the available fourteen-inch-by-twenty-inch space to locate the chosen word/typeface. And then again to discover in what direction the word should face. And finally yet another flip to discover whether the word should be perceived intact or have missing parts, or "whether it is in a state of nonstructural disintegration." And so forth.

The effect of such chance operations, as always in Cage, is to divorce the details from any personal taste and then to give all the elements, whether whole words or just parts of letters, equal status in the work. Because he had nothing particular to say about Duchamp, it is scarcely surprising that the words behind the first Plexigram, say, should be "agglutination, voltaic, wild rubber, trichoid, agrological, exstipulate, suc-, undershrub, shawl, advanced, moccasin flowers," and so forth. He used similar aleatory methods to collect images from a picture encyclopedia.

Regardless of what individual words, letters, parts of letters, or images appear, such randomly chosen and randomly deconstructed images on Plexiglas are likely to produce an evenly distributed, all-over field of linguistic/visual materials devoid of syntactic connection or semantic connotations. If you distribute different collections of such materials on a succession of eight Plexiglas sheets stacked vertically on a single base, the chaotic effect is multiplied. What you see is a three-dimensional field that can be viewed both horizontally and vertically, with the possibility of discovering continuously varying relationships between elements on the front Plexigrams and those in the back. As the Plexigrams can be removed from their slots, you are also free to reorder them. It is not for nothing, I've always assumed, that in its verticality and its inscriptional style the entire work resembles a gravestone. (Cage also derived from this process two lithographs on black paper, lesser works in my judgment; they too have a dense, all-over field reminiscent of Pollock.)

His principal collaborator on this project was the graphic designer Calvin Sumsion. "I composed it. I wrote it," Cage told an interviewer. "First we worked together, then I was able to tell him to do something, and then he would send back the work completed. Albers has used such methods—hasn't he with his own work?—or he gives it to some craftsman to do. Many artists now, when they don't know a particular craft, learn how to tell a craftsman what to do." Cage's other associates on this project included the lithographic printers Irwin Hollander and Fred Genis.

Cage insisted Duchamp would have appreciated the fragmentation of language. "I found a remark of his, after I had done the work, that he often enjoyed looking at signs that were weathered because, where letters were missing, it was fun to figure out what the words were before they had weathered. The reason, in my work, that they are weathered is because he had died. So every word is in a state of disintegration." Like the truest Cagean work, *Not Wanting to Say Anything* is extreme, not only in its refusal to say but in the use of three-dimensional verbal-visual materials. As the art critic Barbara Rose put it, "The result of Cage's investigation surely proves that the artist asserts himself even in negation."

Some of Cage's compositions are minimal, having much less content than art previously had, while others are maximal, having a spectacular abundance of artistic activity. Especially in comparison to the visual art following it, *Not Wanting to Say Anything About Marcel* represents his maximal imagination at its visual best.

• The Song Books Score (1970)

While appreciative of Cage's work as both a visual artist and a maker of esthetically special books (such as *Notations* [1969]), I'd not until recently come to consider Cage's scores apart from their initial purposes as instructions for performance. In this respect the masterpiece, which is really one of the most extraordinary books of its kind produced by any composer ever, is *Song Books*. Published in 1970 in three volumes (the first subtitled "Solos for Voice 3–58," the second "Solos for Voice 59–92," and the third "Instructions"), eight and a half inches high and eleven inches wide, spiral-bound, it is available from Cage's principal music publisher, C. F. Peters, for the curious sum of $207.05 (which does not include the fees required should it ever be recorded or performed before a paying audience).

What the score contains is a wealth of inventive instructions that can be read apart from musical realization; which is to say that the *Song Books* can be appreciated as a book. The instructions fall into four groups: "1) song; 2) song using electronics; 3) theatre; 4) theatre using electronics." By "electronics" Cage meant "wireless throat microphones [that] permit the amplification and transformation of vocal sounds. Contact microphones amplify non-vocal sounds, e.g., activities on a table of typewriter, etc." Imagine them. Typically Cage did not require that the entire score be performed. "Given a total performance time-length, each singer may make a program that will fill it."

Some of the instructions depend upon the clear template provided in the third volume. For instance, "Solo for Voice 3" opens with this instruction for the singer: "Using the map of Concord given, go from Fair Haven Hill (H7) down the river by boat and then inland to the house beyond Blood's (B8). Turn the map so that the path you take suggests a melodic line (read

up and down from left to right). The relation of this line to
voice range is free and this relation may be varied. The tempo
is free." In other words, the performer is asked to sing approximate lines on a map; the reader can hear such lines in her or
his own head.

For texts, Cage provided sequences of words drawn primarily from Henry David Thoreau's *Journal* but also from
Marshall McLuhan, Norman O. Brown, Buckminster Fuller,
Marcel Duchamp, and (for the penultimate song) himself.
Sometimes their words are calligraphed, attached to notes; other times they appear set horizontally across the large pages.
Sometimes changing Letraset typography in style and size mid-
sentence, Cage advised, "The different type-faces may be interpreted as changes in intensity, quality, dynamics. Space on the
page is left for the performer to inscribe the vocal path chosen
from the map." For all the deviance from traditional notations
(beginning with the absence of musical staves), these instructions are nonetheless clear.

Other sections have conventional staves, sometimes with
lines of familiar notes (in the G-clef) and other times with
words from the sources noted before. "Solo for Voice 45" has
eighteen pages of separate clusters of notes only, which "may
be used separately from the other solos by a singer or shared by
two to eighteen singers to provide a program of an agreed upon
length." If the latter, one recurring favorite holds that "the best
form of government is no government at all." When the words
are inscribed into staves, as in "Solo for Voice 12," Cage wrote
phrases meant to be spoken in a rough time line prefaced with
this advice:

> Any amount of the material may be sung (including
> none). No part once sung is to be repeated. Each page
> has six systems [staves]. The time-length of each system
> is free. . . . Notes are of different sizes: generally small,
> medium, and large. A small note is either *ppp, pp, p* in
> the dynamic range or short in duration or both. A

medium note is either mp, mf in the dynamic range or medium in duration or both. A large note is either *f, ff, fff* in the dynamic range or long in duration or both. The possible interpretations are many.

What he made are parts that are infinitely combinable.

Another form of *Song Books* scoring has dots appearing in four channels between five horizontal lines running from end to end for successive pages. In "Solo for Voice 11" the dots within these channels congregate toward the top of the crosswise channels: "The vertical space gives voice range. Therefore, the notes are all in the upper range. Use free vocalise." Above the horizontal lines are numerals that govern the use of electronic accompaniments: "Large numbers (1–64) are to be related to the number of available dials. . . . Smaller numbers (1–12) indicate dial positions as on a chronometer." Therefore, the appearance of a new number in the continuing horizontal sequence requires some sort of decisive change in sound amplification. You can almost imagine it.

Some pages have just numerals in various typefaces, each preceded by a plus or a minus sign. Cage instructed: "To prepare for a performance, the actor will make a numbered list of verbs (actions) and/or nouns (things) not to exceed sixty-four with which he or she is willing to be involved and which are theatrically feasible (those may include stage properties, clothes, etc.; actions may be "real" or mimed, etc.)." If the performers make less than sixty-four options, they should interpret the scored numbers by consulting *I Ching* tables that Cage provided in the third volume. He continued: "The minus and plus signs may be given any significance that the performer finds useful. For instance, a minus sign may mean 'beginning with' or 'taking off,' etc.; a plus sign may mean 'going on' or 'putting on,' etc." For all the allowance of variation, the indeterminate instructions are designed to produce musical results that will strike sophisticated ears as uniquely Cagean.

In another scored structure, the top half is the mirror image of its bottom half. In the middle of one of these, "Solo for Voice 33," is a text in French (from Erik Satie). The shape functions as a prescription for the production of sound: "Let the upper and lower extremes for the symmetrical shape relate to the upper and lower extremes of voice register. Let horizontal space relate to time." This solo, unlike most others, has a prescribed duration, in this case of two minutes and thirty seconds. Some solos depend upon breath inhaled and exhaled (and thus electronically amplified). As some depend upon the map of Concord noted before, others must be seen with a line portrait of Thoreau that is bound into the third volume. From time to time Cage even encouraged performers to draw upon such earlier scores of his as *Atlas Eclipticalis* (1961–1962) or *Winter Music* (1957). "Solo for Voice 32" has a strictly theatrical instruction that is simply written: "Go off-stage at a normal speed, hurrying back somewhat later." You need not read music to appreciate this writing, though you must follow directions and cross-references.

He concluded specific suggestions with the advice that "a virtuoso performance will include a wide variety of styles of singing and vocal production," the counterconventional form of each part thus contributing to the counterconventional theme of the whole, both of which are designed to encourage not one vocal possibility but many. Produced in the wake of *Notations*, which was also an anthology of possibilities, *Song Books* becomes the richest introduction to Cage's creative inventions of the 1950s and 1960s. Lest his politics be mistaken, he proposed early in the piece posting not the red flag of Communism but the equally traditional "black flag of Anarchy."

Some version of the *Song Books* should be made available in a more economical edition, much as classical scores are reprinted in bookstore "trade" editions. It is historically important, not only because no one was writing scores like this before Cage began but also because many have done so since.

One reason for ignorance of this score is that recordings of it are scarce. Joan La Barbara recorded only three sections, while the Schola Cantorum Stuttgart's realizations of a few other parts accompany a Wergo recording of Cage's declaiming *Empty Words*. American Music/Theatre Group's (Neely Bruce's) evening-length *Song Books* production, which I saw at Wesleyan University early in 1988, ranks in my mind among the great Cage performances; I'd love to have a recording.

Especially compared to other scores of his, which often follow only a single structural line, *Song Books* is a wealth of uniquely Cagean processes that page by page offer a succession of surprises. That is one reason why it can be *read* with pleasure.

• Empty Words (1974–1975)

> I was always impressed by John Cage's statement that when you build a structure that strong you can accept all sorts of things into it.
>
> —Robert Dunn, in an interview with Don McDonagh, *The Rise and Fall and Rise of Modern Dance* (1970)

*L*anguage was the base of much of John Cage's work in the 1970s and 1980s—language that is meant to be read and spoken without specific pitches (that would, by contrast, make the words song). These works are not essays, or even antiessays, like his earlier "Lecture on Nothing" (1959). As literary creations these later works are generically closer to poetry than to essays or fiction in that they represent compressions of language rather than extensions into narrative (fiction) or definitions of extrinsic reality (essays). Cage's first departure in this poetic direction was the essayistic "Diaries," produced in the late sixties, which are, in essence, a formally rigorous and typographically various shorthand for miscellaneous remarks. Three of these "Diaries" appeared in *A Year from Monday* (1967), and in the course of reviewing this book I suggested that Cage's work with words had not been as radical as his work with sound. Rather than dispute me, Cage remembered my criticisms (and repeatedly reminded me that he had) and moved ahead. He made a sequence of cleverly structured visual poems in memory of his friend Marcel Duchamp, *Not Wanting To Say Anything About Marcel* (1969), and then *Sixty-two Mesostics re Merce Cunningham* (1971), a series of vertically organized words that exploit the unique possibilities of rub-off lettering. He developed, in *Mureau* (1971), a nonsyntactic prose that was based not, like the "Diaries," upon his own experience and his own language, but upon words drawn from

Henry David Thoreau's *Journal*. He further extended this line of work in his 1979 book, *Empty Words*.

Empty Words contains expository essays on "The Future of Music" and "How the Piano Came to Be Prepared." Both of these are of interest to followers of Cage's musical thinking. Another section, ostensibly about both the choreographer Merce Cunningham and food, illustrates Cage's genius for story-telling. However, most of this book contains language con-structions that must be called "poetry," partly because they are not prose but mostly because they cannot be persuasively clas-sified as anything else. Because these poems are radically unlike everything else in American writing today, it is scarcely surpris-ing that they are rarely discussed by "poetry critics" and never mentioned in the current surveys of American literature.

Notwithstanding his advocacy of "chance" and artistic freedom, Cage was a poetic formalist who invented alternative ways of *structuring* language. One device is the mesostic. Whereas the familiar acrostic has a word running down the left-hand margin of several lines, the mesostic has a recogniz-able word running down the middle. In Cagean practice, this vertical word is usually the name of a friend—Merce Cunning-ham, Jasper Johns, Norman O. Brown. Within this mesostic constraint, Cage makes concise statements:

> not Just
>   gArdener
> morelS
>   coPrini
> morEls
> cop Rini.
>   not Just hunter:
> cutting dOwn
> ailan tHus
>   cuttiNg down
> ailanthuS.

The title piece of *Empty Words* is a four-part poem drawn from Henry David Thoreau's remarks about music and sound. Cage copied relevant passages out of Thoreau's journals and then subjected them to *I Ching*–aided chance processes that, in effect, scrambled and combined them, eventually producing a nonsyntactic pastiche of Thoreau's language:

> speaksix round and longer than
> the shelloppressed and
> now ten feet high heroTheclosely isor
> have looked wellthat and spruces
> the and a darker line below it

This stanza comes from the first page of the first part, which contains phrases, words, syllables, and letters (characters) from Thoreau. The second part of "Empty Words" contains just his words, syllables, and letters; the third part just syllables and letters; and the fourth part just letters.

Cage's long poem "Empty Words" is less about Thoreau than about sound, or the sound of language about sound, compressed and recombined; reading it is not about assuaging our powers of literary understanding but about challenging and expanding them. This is rigorously Platonic poetry that takes initially spiritual literature and recomposes it into a yet more ethereal realm. In my opinion, "Empty Words" is better heard than read.

Scarcely contented with past poetic inventions, Cage developed a series of conceptually ambitious schemes for extracting language from James Joyce's multilingual masterpiece, *Finnegans Wake*. In the initial scheme, Cage worked from the beginning of Joyce's book to its end, extracting words that contain letters that fit into a mesostic structure based upon the name "James Joyce." Since the first *J* in *Finnegans Wake* appears in the word "nathandjoe," Cage took out that word and then, by a decision of taste, decided to take as well the three adjacent words to the left of it (ignoring those to the right). For the *a* of "James" he selected only the article (and implicitly decided against both sets of words adjacent to it). The next *m* appears in the word "malt"; the next *e* in "Jhem"; and the next *s* in "Shen." Thus, Cage's opening stanza reads:

wroth with twone nathandJoe
A
Malt
jhEm
Shen

It is a simple measure of Cage's originality that nobody ever made poetry like this before—the method is, like so much of his work, at once sensible and nutty. To my mind, *Writing Through Finnegans Wake* is interesting in part because it is so audaciously innovative; it succeeds in part because it recycles James Joyce. Hearing Cage read it aloud, with sensitive precision, was a special pleasure.

Empty Words contains only the second of Cage's workings with the *Wake*; the first, longer Joyce piece appeared initially as a special issue of the *James Joyce Quarterly* and has since been reissued as a book, *Writing Through Finnegans Wake* (1978). Both Cage *Wake* pieces appear together in a third book, a large-format signed and limited edition titled *Writings Through Finnegans Wake* (1978) (note the plural in the first word). Reproducing Cage's manuscript in its original size, this sumptuously produced volume is superior to the reduced versions, even though its high price is amenable, alas, primarily to libraries and collectors of Cage's visual art.

Cage described *Empty Words* as progressing, over its four parts, from literature to music, and it seems to me that both this work and its Joycean successor finally realized an identity between the two traditional arts. *Text-sound* is the epithet I use to define language works that cohere primarily in terms of sound rather than syntax or semantics; and Cage, as a literary musician, was clearly a master of that domain. On the other hand, because both *Empty Words* and *Writings Through Finnegans Wake* are language-based, they fit snugly into the great American tradition of poetry that realizes an eccentric innovation in the machinery of the art—a radical change not in meaning or in sensibility but in the materials indigenous to poetry: language, line, syntax, and meter. (In this sense Cage's principal poetic precursors are Whitman, Cummings, and Gertrude Stein.) Considered in this way, Cage was not a literary curiosity but an exemplary American poet.

I spoke with Cage about how he created these unusual literary works, including *Mureau* and *Empty Words*; here's some of his thoughts.

Having agreed to write a text about electronic music, and having noticed that HDT—that's Thoreau—listened to sound as electronic composers listen to it, not just to musical sounds but to noises and ambient sound generally, it occurred to me that making a chance-determined mix of his remarks in the *Journal* about sound, silence, and music would make a text relevant to electronic music. Therefore, I gave it the title *Mu*(music)*reau*(Thoreau). I went through the index of the Dover edition of the *Journal*, and I noticed every occurrence in the index of anything that could be remotely thought to be connected with music, and then I listed all of those appearances; then I subjected it all to chance operations in terms of sentences, phrases, words, syllables, and letters. I made a permutation of those five possibilities, so that it could be each of the five alone, or in any groups of two, or any groups of three, or any groups of four, or finally all five.

In gathering the original material for Mureau, *you took phrases out of Thoreau and sentences out of Thoreau and words out of Thoreau.*
First I listed all the things having to do with sound. Then I asked, what it was of all those permuted possibilities I was

looking for, whether I was looking for all five together or a group of four of them, or a group of three or a group of two or one. And when I knew what I was doing, my next question was for how many events was I doing it? And the answer could be anywhere from one to sixty-four. Let's say I got twenty-three. Then if I knew that I was looking for twenty-three events which were any of these five, then I asked of this five which is the first one. Which is the second? Which is the third? So I knew finally what I was doing. And then when I knew what I was doing, I did it.

How did you decide to begin work, in the case of Mureau?
I wanted to make a text that would have four parts, and it was written for a magazine in Minneapolis called *Synthesis*. And they were written to be columns. I was a columnist for the magazine. I don't think of these texts as lectures. They were conceived as columns, initially, and if you'll notice, the columns have different widths. I did that on purpose.

I was continuing *Mureau*, but extending it beyond Thoreau's remarks about sound and music to the whole of the *Journal*. To begin with, I omitted sentences, and I thought of *Empty Words* as a transition from literature to music.

In the first notebooks of *Empty Words*, each part is called a lecture. It was something to be read aloud, and therefore I made it a length that some people would consider excessive; I made a length of two hours and a half for each lecture.

How did you determine that?
Most people consider this excessive, and they don't want me to give it as a lecture. I think that's because the average lecture, say in a college, should be forty minutes.

Why did you make your own lectures nearly four times as long?
I had been very impressed by an experience I had in Japan, in 1964, of going to a Buddhist service. We went to an evening

lecture there that went on for hours and hours, and we had been warned that it was going to be tiresome. I was with Merce Cunningham and the Dance Company. It was very cold, and we were not protected by any warmth. They had told us it would be uncomfortable and long, but we were told also that we didn't have the right to leave once we had decided that we wanted to stay. So we all suffered through it, and it went on and on, for something like six hours.

And then a few days later, or maybe it was on another trip to Japan, I was in a Zen temple in Kyoto. When I was invited to go to an early morning Buddhist service, I did. I noticed that after a lengthy service they opened the doors of the temple, and you heard the sounds coming in from the outside. So, putting these two things together, the long night business and then the dawn of the opening of the doors, I thought of the opening of the doors occurring at dawns and making four lectures and the fourth would begin at dawn with the opening of the doors to the outer world so that the sounds would come in—because you see it was a transition from literature to music, and my notion of music has always been ambient sound anyway, silence.

This was Thoreau's notion of music too, you see. Music is continual, he said; it's only listening which is intermittent. I can read to you from the *Journal* long passages written when he was twenty-one years old, if you please, or twenty-two at the most, on the subject of silence. He said silence was a sphere, and sounds were bubbles on its surface. Isn't that beautiful?

So your idea of Empty Words *was a lecture heard for ten hours. . . .*
And you'd have half-hour intermissions between the parts. So you'd first have to find out when dawn was coming, the way fishermen do, and then you'd figure back and you'd finally know when the lecture was to begin. So, with three half-hour

intermissions, you'd therefore have to begin eleven and a half hours before dawn. I then thought, probably because of Margaret Mead, that those intermissions should include food, that people eating together is an important thing and that is basic to Margaret Mead's notion of ritual.

So that's how the record of Empty Words *should ideally be heard as well?*
Yes, during that length of time, if one does listen to it over that length of time, there should be periods when one stops listening and has something to eat.

Why does it have the title Empty Words?
It comes from a description of the Chinese language that was given to me by William McNaughton, who has made marvelous translations of both Japanese and Chinese texts. The Chinese language, he said, has "full words" and "empty words." Full words are words that are nouns or verbs or adjectives or adverbs. We don't know in Chinese which of these a full word is. The word is so full that it could be any of them. For instance, the word "red" is an adjective. It could be—I'm hypothesizing now—it could be the same as the verb to blush, to turn red. It could be the same as ruby or cherry, if those were names for red. It is a full word because it has several semantic possibilities. It can mean any one of those things. An empty word, by contrast, is a connective or a pronoun—a word that refers to something else. Or it has no meaning by itself. For example, if I say to you "it," that would be an empty word. But if I said "microphone," that would be a full word. I would like with my title to suggest the emptiness of meaning that is characteristic of musical sounds. That is to say they exist by themselves—that when words are seen from a musical point of view, they are all empty.

You had this notion of Empty Words *in your mind at the beginning. You also had the notion of developing a piece that would be away from something that was just read on the page to something that would be performed, as it approaches music.*

The approach to music is made by steadily eliminating one of the aspects of language, so that as we start Lecture One of *Empty Words*, we have no sentences. Though they did exist in *Mureau*, now they're gone. In the second one, the phrases are gone, and in the third part the words are gone, except those that have only one syllable. And in the last one, everything is gone but letters and silences.

So you've had a further reduction within the piece. But let me go back a step. Were the same compositional methods used in manipulating the material from Thoreau in Mureau *as were used in* Empty Words?

Yes.

Then why is Mureau *generally written continuously, like prose?*

Mureau was a column to be printed in a magazine, and *Empty Words* is a lecture. In fact, the whole thing is, through chance operations, put in the form of stanzas. That is to say that one part of it is separated from another part. And the parts were determined by the appearance of a period following whatever word, syllable, or letters that were chance-obtained.

Let me go back to the question of the four major Sections, or "Lectures" as you call them. When did one of them end?

When there were 4,000 events at least. In the case of the First Lecture, there are 4,060, and the reason for that excessive number is this: when I got to making the 3,997th event, I threw a sixty-four, and it took me up to 4,060.

So you did the first 4,060 lines, and thereby finished Part One of Empty Words. *In Part Two, you continued with*

*your method but you removed the possibility of phrases.
And continued to do the same thing. And in* Empty Words,
Three, *you removed the possibility of words, so you had just
syllables and letters, and then in* Four, *just letters.*

I had one further idea, but I guess that it doesn't apply to the
recording. That was to sit in profile for the first one. Then face
the audience for the second one. To sit in profile again but on
the other side for the third. And then with my back to the audience for the fourth. And it was actually at Naropa that I sat
with my back to the audience, and they became infuriated.

*Each of the four works comes with a preface—actually each
section has a preface that incorporates the prefaces of its
predecessor, until there is a four-part preface to the last one.
What are they meant to do?*

All the information, all the answers to all the questions, such as
those you now are asking me, are given as conscientiously as I
can in these introductions. I tried to imagine what it is anyone
would want to know and then I give them that information in
the introduction, but not in any logical sequence.

How were these prefaces written?

The first thing I did was find out how many words I had at my
disposal for the first remark or for the first answer. One, two,
three, plus two plus two plus one, eleven. I had eleven words.
Now I thought, well, what shall I say. And it occurred to me to
say at the beginning how it was that I came to be in connection
with Thoreau. That seemed to be a reasonable beginning.

*And it reads: "Wendell Berry: Passages outloud from Thore-
au's* Journal (Port Royal, Kentucky, 1967)." *That's eleven
words.*

It was at that time and in that place that Wendell Berry picked
up a copy of the *Journal*—we had just had dinner together; I
was in his home. He read passages out loud to me. And the
moment he did that was the next remark, which has thirty-four

words: "Realized I was starved for Thoreau (just as in 1954 when I moved from New York City to Stony Point, I had realized I was starved for nature; took to walking in the woods)." I thought I should have said after that, but I didn't have room, that I took to reading Thoreau just as I had taken to walking in the woods; but I thought that once I'd said it in that way—that since I realized I was starved for Thoreau, I think you'd realize I started reading the *Journal*.

And then, "Agreed to write work for voices (Song books)" and so forth. The third line of the first preface seems like a very long statement, but then you have a very short statement about "Syntax: arrangement of the army," which is a reference to Norman O. Brown's sensitive remark that conventional syntax, in its lining up of words, represents the militarization of language.
These are answers to possible questions about *Empty Words*.

Admittedly in skeletal form. You also explain here how you use the I Ching *in this piece.*
And do you know what? I was able—you see, time passes and I get involved in different projects and I had forgotten—and I had for years been reading Part Three. Every time anyone asked me to give a lecture I would read that. And I forgot how I had read Part One. Or Part Two. And when I tried to do it for the record, I found I couldn't. I didn't know how. So I thought, how will I find out. Then I realized that I'd answered all these questions in the introduction. So I got out the Introduction to Part Three and it says there, "Searching (outloud) for a way to read. Changing frequency. Going up and then going down; going to extremes. Establish (I, II) stanza's time. That brings about a variety of tempi (short stanzas become slow; long become fast)." I counted the number of stanzas and divided the total length, two hours and one-half, by the number of stanzas and thus determined that most of the stanzas in Part One would be forty seconds long. Some, the longer ones, would be a little longer.

In your own score for your readings, what you've done is timed when you should begin each stanza, and beside you as you read is a stopwatch. You have other marks suggesting where words should be divided into syllables. Let's say you have a stanza, like the twenty-third, which has twelve lines. If you have only forty seconds, you'd have to speak quite quickly to get through that.

Right. A stanza that long has to be read very fast. See, it has forty-four seconds actually. In order to make the thing come out evenly with two hours and one-half, I made a complicated but symmetrical arrangement, and I gave a few more seconds to the longer stanzas so that reading them became more practical. Not a great many, but, like, four seconds. I was delighted to learn how to read this and to learn this from my introduction.

That is why those introductions are so important, not only to readers but to you.

There was a criticism of this text by our dear friend Jackson Mac Low in that interesting critical magazine called L=A=N=G=U=A=G=E. Jackson said that though he enjoyed hearing *Empty Words*, he had no interest in reading it. He found that he never picked it up to read. The only reason he doesn't pick up the text is that he doesn't know how to read it. If he knew how to read it, he would immediately become fascinated by it. I've shown that with the recording, and I've found it out from reading the introduction, that the moment you set up the stanza time and then follow that, timed with a stopwatch, then immediately you become fascinated with the whole problem of reading it. That's the musical problem.

Let's go back to the very beginning of Part One, "notAt evening." You have that section marked for forty seconds and the one after that for eighty seconds on the stopwatch and then for one hundred twenty seconds and then the one after that for two minutes. Is it your notion that one should read each part for forty seconds?

No. The forty seconds will include your reading of those lines. And anything else that's in those forty seconds is silence, which is to say ambient sounds.

Therefore, I look at those first three lines, and I have forty seconds to think about them, while I glance at the stopwatch to measure myself. When I look at the next two lines, I get forty more seconds to consider them.
No, no. You read them. You've been advised to do this by James Joyce in connection with *Finnegans Wake*. He says the book was not to be read silently, but should be read out loud.

Out loud to oneself?
Yes. Not just looked at but said out loud.

So just as a Bach score is meant to be taken to the piano to play, Empty Words *is meant to be taken with a stopwatch and read aloud to oneself. Or to one's friends, whoever's there. If someone asks you, as I had planned to do, what is the difference between hearing it and reading it, you would reply that there is no reading without hearing—you haven't read the text unless you've heard it.*
   So, therefore, one can in eleven hours have the experience, the full experience, of Empty Words *entirely by oneself.*
It's conceivable, don't you think, that if someone initiated such a search as that, and such a discipline, that he might discover another way to read it.

I was going to ask about that. Once you've recorded it, haven't you prejudiced its sound, to most of us; and your answer would be, no, I've given you only my way to do it, but that's not necessarily going to be your way to do it.
   What then do I hear when I hear you reading it, in performance or on the record? What would I hear when I hear myself reading it?
I think that this is a question that changes with each listener.

There are people, as you know, who are color blind. So there must be people who just have no interest in sound whatsoever and who are insensitive to everything in language but "meaning."

And they would say that in Empty Words *they had heard nothing.*
And then there may be, on the other hand, people who are musically inclined who are not so oppressed by meaning. Or the need to have meaning. There are very many ways to hear something. I'll put it this other way: I think one should pay attention to everything when one does anything. And if one is listening one should be attentive to all the various characteristics of sound and language that there are, because we are dealing with a complex situation, a transition from language to music, or from literature to music.

Is it then comparable to the experience, which we've all had, of being in a room where everybody's talking in a language we don't know and we thus try to appreciate the music of the language itself?
Someone speaking a foreign language, except that the language here is not entirely foreign. It's from Thoreau. When it gets inscrutable, because it does with letters and syllables and so on, people remark to me frequently that it sounds like old English—something else they don't understand. What's interesting are all the variety of things that happen: the sounds, the rhythm, the inflections, the this, the that—all these things. You can never tell when something's going to set your faculties working.

So, indeed, it is meant to remind you of other things as well.
It's unavoidable, don't you think, Richard? Because the human mind is more complex than a computer; the moment something comes into it, it touches bells, it rings bells, with regard to the rest of the mind. And everybody's mind is like this, even the

man in the street, who's not supposed to be bright. But he is very bright. He's brighter than a computer.

Now it seems to me that Empty Words *demands of us a kind of discipline in that, as it goes from Part One to Part Four, it does get harder and harder to listen to, as the intentional verbal or vocal content gets sparser and sparser.*
This varies with people. Very frequently someone gets up and leaves during the course of the reading, but at the same performance someone will come to me after the reading and say that I could have gone on forever. As far as he was concerned, it would have been a pleasure. And this is true of Part Three which I've been reading so frequently. Part Four, well, offered problems to the audience at Naropa. And part of it came, I think, from my sitting with my back to them, for I'd no sooner begun to read than they began an uproar. And I had to be protected physically by quite a redoubtable group of people, including Allen Ginsberg.

How large an audience was there?
Three thousand people, and they went into a state of disenchantment—complete disenchantment.

How many stayed until the end?
I would say at least three-quarters of the audience. And it went on for two hours and a half.

And you had your back turned. Were you amplified in any way?
Yes. Some of the silences were twelve and thirteen minutes long. After the performance I promised them that I would go through a period of self-examination, and I counseled them to do likewise, since we had gotten along so badly together that night.

I first heard you perform Part Four at St. Marks Church in the spring of 1975. Then you spoke it; since then, I've heard that you've developed a singing style for it.

A chanting, yes. Well, it was part of this reexamination that I counseled the audience at Naropa to do. And I decided to make this text more musical than I had.

And this decision came after your Naropa reading?
It was for the recording, actually. And now that I've made it, and now that I've done it, I enjoy it, and I will in the immediate future, when I'm asked to give a lecture, do this chant.

Just for Part Four. Does it bother you when people walk out?
No, it doesn't bother me because they are the ones who are walking out. I myself am staying.

Does it bother you when people heckle, as apparently they did at Naropa?
I can't say that it doesn't bother me, but I can say this: that it does not bother me to such an extent that I stop what I'm doing. What I'm doing is so exigent, so demanding, it requires me to pay attention to everything I am doing. I don't have much time to be bothered by the people who are walking out.

How many times have you performed Empty Words *around the United States? Twenty times? Forty times?*
More. I don't know. In Europe, too. You see it's a text that, since it doesn't mean anything, can be read in a foreign country. This is one of the advantages of nonsyntactical writing.

That's an advantage of music as well.
That it moves toward a whole world.

Have you ever read it to an audience that has copies of the text in front of them, as people possessing the record will?
I think that will happen more, because *Empty Words* is my next book and the book will be included in the package with the recording [that has not yet appeared].

Does it help? Is it a good idea?
I think it will help, yes.

Do you recommend it?
It's according to whether you're the sort of person who likes to read the score while listening to the music.

On this projected recording, Maryanne Amacher is your collaborator. How did you conceive of her role and how would you describe what she is doing?
I've done a number of works involving environmental sound, ambient sound. One of them was *Score with Parts* (1974), which I did for the St. Paul Chamber Orchestra. I used the environmental sound of dawn at Stony Point, New York, where I had written the music, and David Behrman made that recording, and he made another recording for me for the piece called *Etcetera*. Again it was ambient sound not at dawn, just anytime during the day. It was composed for a dance that Merce did in Paris called *Un Jour ou Deux* [*One Day or Two*]. And when I was invited by the CBC to make a bicentennial piece called *Lecture on the Weather*, I thought also of asking David Behrman to make a recording of wind, rain, and thunder for the whole thing. Somehow he didn't receive the letter that I sent him. He was at York University in Toronto, and it went to the wrong part of the university. It just wasn't received. Finally I telephoned him, but he was then committed and couldn't do it and thought I should engage Maryanne Amacher, for, he said, she did the best recordings of ambient environmental sounds. I knew that her work was very beautiful. I had heard it, and I agreed with him immediately. So I engaged her to do that and her friend Luis Frangella, an Argentinian, to make a film of lightning with the drawings of Thoreau as the flashes of light. So that Thoreau himself became the thunder. And the speakers preferably would be people who had given up their American citizenship and were becoming Canadians, so it was a dark

bicentennial piece. Like Thoreau, it criticized the government and its history. And the twelve speakers are speaking quotations from the "Essay on Civil Disobedience," the *Journal*, and *Walden*, according to chance operations.

Which are coherent quotations, or fragments, as in Mureau *or* Empty Words?
They're coherent, but they're so superimposed that you can't understand anything. It's the same experience you would have if you had twelve radios going at once. Or if you had tuned between stations and could hear several going at once.

• Europera (1987): Before and After

I.

> Louis Armstrong or any other good jazz musician of that period would take a theme and start improvising. He would pay his respects to *Aida*, any number of operas, light opera, and religious music. All of this came out in the improvisation. It assumes possession and it recasts. There is a kind of irreverent reverence that Americans are likely to have for materials of the past.
>
> —Ralph Ellison,
> in an interview with the author (1965)

*I*n his mid-seventies, John Cage wrote his first opera. "I was asked to write an opera, and I have never written one," John Cage told an interviewer. "It means a lot of work. It means a theater piece with all those singers. And you see, I've come to the desire to free each person in the performance from anyone like a conductor. Instead, what I want the opera to be is a collage of sorts, of a pulverized sort, of European opera; and my title, I think, is excellent. It's *Europera*, which is the words 'Europe' and 'opera' put together." As one of Cage's best verbal inventions, this coinage also sounds like "Your Opera," which is to say everyone's opera.

What Cage did, armed with a commission from the Frankfurt Opera, was to ransack the repertoire of traditional (i.e., European) operas that were no longer protected by copyright; from their scores he selected instrumental parts, each no more than sixteen measures long, that could, by chance processes, be reassembled differently for each performance. To get these fragments, Cage and his assistant, Andrew Culver, went to the basement library of the Metropolitan Opera, where they pulled pages at random to be photocopied. Then, in performance, parts appropriate to each instrument were to be assigned to approximately two dozen musicians (flutists, say, getting a miscellany of flute music), each of whom was to have music different from his colleagues'. Thus, motifs from different operas would be heard from different instruments simultaneously.

To "write" the singers' "arias," Cage began with the information that there are nineteen different categories of operatic voices (for sopranos alone, for instance, coloratura, lyric coloratura, lyric, lyric spinto, and dramatic), so he asked his sponsors for one of each. The nineteen singers would be allowed to select which out-of-copyright arias they might sing, but only in the performance itself would they find out when and where (or if). The singers were to follow not a conductor but digital time displays that would signal their entrances; questions of duration and dynamics at any time were to be left to chance. It was possible for several arias, each from a different opera, to be sung at once, to instrumental accompaniment(s) culled from yet other operas. About recognizing such arias, Cage wrote, with characteristic wit, "Ah-hah effects will in all probability occur more frequently here than in the case of the orchestra parts and above all have a much stronger impact."

The opera's costumes were likewise drawn from disparate sources. From the library of New York's Fashion Institute of Technology, a few blocks from his New York studio, Cage borrowed a multivolumed encyclopedia. By certain chance operations to which he was devoted, he found individual designs that were photographed; slides were then forwarded to Frankfurt for fabrication. These clothes were assigned to individual singers without reference to what they would sing or do onstage. It was here, more than anywhere else, that Cage dramatized his pulverizing objectives. As none of the performers was to wear an embellished costume that would invidiously distinguish him or her as a "star," all performers were to be equal.

For theatrical decor, Cage extended his esthetic principle. From a wealth of opera pictures found in Frankfurt libraries, he selected images from various dimensions of operatic experience (singers, composers, stage sets, animals, etc.) and had them enlarged and painted, only in black-and-white, for the flats. These flats were to be mechanically brought onstage from left or right or above with an arbitrariness reminiscent of the changing backdrops in the Marx Brothers' *A Night at the Opera*. Once a flat or prop was no longer needed, it was simply to be laid to rest beside the performing area, visibly contributing to the chaotic mise-en-scène.

In a booklet prepared for the original performance is this further explanation: "A computer program, compiled by chance operations, controls the lighting process. It only makes use of the black-and-white range [except for two passages of color] to avoid any fundamental modification in the chromatic value of the costumes," which is to say that the lighting could not be intentionally manipulated either to focus the audience's attention or to give one performer more presence than the others. One subsequent innovation that could be used in any later performance is a variable computer-assisted system that can generate 3,500 separate lighting cues to 180 different lamps—an average of twenty-six autonomous lighting changes per minute, thereby making the stage illumination not only serendipitous but radically different from performance to performance.

Once Cage assembled this wealth of independent elements, he had to devise a scheme for proceeding in time. In what is perhaps his most audacious move he went to the second edition of *Webster's Unabridged Dictionary*, looking at chance-selected two-page spreads until he found listings that suggested actions. In the Frankfurt performance, one aria was sung from inside a garbage pail, others from inside a coffin and inside a bathtub. Singers arrived onstage in a Jeep or inside the belly of a fish. The time available for each action was determined by chance operations; so were the moments of entrance and exit. Nothing relates to anything else, except by coincidence.

Because it was possible for individual performers to be assigned tasks that could not be done alone, there were several athletic supers, so-called, onstage to assist them. When a singer was stretched out from his normal height to twelve feet, a super attached the cables that executed the illusion. The supers also installed a cloud and then climbed up and down the ladder attached to it. A final pseudoarbitrary decision was that the performance happening prior to the interim intermission, officially called *Europera 1*, would have ten singers and be ninety minutes long; the part after the intermission, *Europera 2*, would have the remaining nine singers and be forty-five minutes long.

The book-length score must be seen to be believed. After Cage's single-page introduction is a geometric chart that divides the stage into sixty-four rectangles. Then come a series of pages with times running down the left-hand margin. In "flat cues," say, across from each notation of time are shorthand indications of individual moves for the supply of flats. Similar time charts inform the action. Were this score posted to a country that censors mail, it would surely be examined for months. "Music," let alone opera, was never before written like this.

"Originally I thought to have the music [of *Europera*] be the music in the repertoire of operas of that particular opera house, so that both the sets and the costumes would already exist," he told Ellsworth Snyder, the interviewer mentioned before. "They would simply be collaged in a different way from conventionally. So instead of having one opera, you'd have them all in one evening. And it's a very nice idea and relatively practical, but it turns out that operas—I was told, as I never go to the opera, of course—I was told that the opera had become quite modern, the sets were not what I imagined, and the costumes were too often not what I would think they had been in the past." From these realizations came the decisions to use music that had aged out of copyright and both new costumes and new sets (rather than those already in storage).

"Rather than have the lighting focused on the activity, I would like to have the lighting done by means of chance operations. I'll probably find out what is the minimum light, so that the singers won't fall down or something. And what would be the maximum lighting. Then to play between those, with what must be very good technology now. And that won't be too difficult. I'm disconnecting not only the lighting from the singers but the costumes from the roles and the background from the activity, and I'm going to introduce a number of what I think of as stage effects, things happening, so that the whole performance will be like not a choreography involving a dance, but still a kind of movement in this space without benefit of a plot."

Europera was designed to open at the Frankfurt Opera on November 15, 1987. However, three days before the premiere, that regal theater was gutted by a fire attributed to a vagrant looking for food. Instead, it opened on December 12 in the smaller Schauspielhaus. Tickets were so hard to obtain that I suspect, a generation from now, the number of people saying they were there will be twice the number of seats. (Several months later, in Sweden, I heard a critic for a daily newspaper there stop a conversation about something else to boast that, yes, he got a precious ticket.) The American premiere came the following summer at SUNY-Purchase.

In the original performance was another innovation that was not duplicated in New York. From traditional operatic plot summaries, Cage extracted sentences, replacing specific names with pronouns like *he* and *she*. These sentences were scrambled to produce twelve different pseudosummaries, each two paragraphs long (to coincide with the two acts), none of which had any intentional connection to what was happening on the stage. This is the second half of the twelfth:

He lusts after her; she had died, his only hope of redemption. In his despondency he maintains his reserve, accepts the bird. He fulfills the second part of the witches' prophecy: They rescue him quickly. He loses his power. He falls prey to another man's wife. Once more he invokes Venus (he is first to admit it); in vain; her life is over. He wishes; he refuses. Thoroughly embittered, he rails.

Into the programs for the Frankfurt performance Cage randomly slipped only *one* of the twelve synopses. As a result, people sitting next to each other had different guides, further contributing to the spirit of general confusion.

However, as few theaters around the world have facilities equal to those in Frankfurt and Purchase, some of the dimensions of *Europera* were scaled down into "chamber versions": *Europeras 3, 4,* and *5.* While the work is audaciously original, it is neither hermetic nor arcane; one could imagine it becoming part of the standard operatic repertoire, mounted from time to time as a charming departure that nonetheless epitomized the opera house tradition—the comic opera to end all operas, comic and otherwise.

My sense of the key to quality in Cage's work is simply that bigger is usually better; the common mark of his greatest works has been an abundance of activity within a frame. Larger works offered Cage the opportunity to explore his tastes for imaginative constraints, alternative materials, and sophisticated laughter. In size and scale, *Europera* belongs to the same class as his *Sonatas and Interludes* (1946–1948), *Williams Mix* (1952), *HPSCHD* (1969), and *Roaratorio* (1979). For all of its contextual innovation, *Europera* nonetheless reflects a compositional principle that has been uniquely Cage's for several decades now—a principle he defines simply as "a circus of independent elements."

Like his earlier masterpieces, *Europera* inspired from the beginning a critical literature. First off the mark were the artistic directors of the Frankfurt Opera, the official "dramaturgs" for this project, Heinz-Klaus Metzger and Rainer Riehn. In the booklet for the original performance, the former wrote, according to the translator, "Clearly, Cage has not written a Romantic opera, but indeed two 'comic' operas—in which the essence of the most European of all traditional forms of theater creates a constellation, namely, the total collage of what comprises the quintessence of those forms and at the same time sublates them critically." Respecting Cage's example of informed pilferage, Riehn composed an aphoristic text drawn entirely from quotations from an unidentified late-eighteenth-century German author (who is actually the writer known only as Novalis, 1772–1801).

The critic of the *Frankfurter Allgemeine Zeitung*, Germany's equivalent of *The New York Times*, found "an acoustical 'musée imaginaire' (referring to André Malraux's characterization of the art book), stuffed full with recitatives, arias and the meaningless phrases of the orchestra parts. Cage thinks like Goethe: 'Dig deeply into the operatic life.'" In the *Stuttgarter Zeitung*, an inspired Horst Koegler wrote, "*I* and *II* can conceivably be reversed—and without difficulty be continued by 'III' and ad infinitum [in this] gigantic operatic revue, a kind of neo-dada which, first of all, represents a test for the quiz capacity for each theater patron." In other words, a work as rich and yet indefinite as *Europera* is likely to prompt an impressive variety of interpretations.

What *Europera* is finally about, to my mind, is the culture of opera, Cage's work being, from its transcriptions of phrases to its libretti, at once a homage and a burlesque, finding a wealth of surprises in the familiar. Its theme could be defined, simply, as the sound of European opera after a wayward American has reprocessed it. Nonetheless, precisely because *Europera* was initially performed in an opera house, with opera professionals (rather than amateurs), on a stage whose curtain went up, it must be judged as opera, not as just a species of anarchist theater (which it also is). Writing in *The Wall Street Journal*, the music critic Mark Swed reported, "For all its wildness, the opera proceeds with an underlying grace and a witty way with operatic clichés, putting them in unexpected contexts, that really was Mozartian in the end." In my judgment, by running innocently amok in European culture, Cage came as close as anyone to writing the Great American Opera, which is to say, a great opera that only an American could make.

What is remarkable is that Cage, after fifty years of ignoring opera, had in this age when "everything has been done" (or "artistic innovation has expired") produced something that is by common consent truly avant-garde, something that makes a significant original contribution to the art. It is also true that by achieving such innovation in his mid-seventies, Cage, who never doubled back (and never rejected earlier work as "too far out"), reaffirmed the expectation that he would be a pioneering presence as long as he continued to work.

II.

It is by surprise, by the important position that has been given to surprise, that the new spirit distinguishes itself from all the literary and artistic movements that have preceded it.

—Guillaume Apollinaire, "The New Spirit and the Poets" (1916)

Regarding his new *Europeras 1* and *2*, John Cage told an interviewer, "It's just so many things going on at once that I think you see different things each time you look at it, if you look at it more than once." Because certain elements in the production, such as entrances and exits of the instrumentalists, would be different from performance to performance, I decided to go to all three performances at the Pepsico Summerfare, in part to see whether the differences were significant but also to discover whether my enthusiasm for Cage would survive after three viewings on four successive days.

As a grand compendium of European opera, *Europera* will test your taste for opera. What you see and what you hear are, simply, the conventions of that art—spacious stage, some typical choreography, formidable performers, costuming, and singing—apart from any specific content. People familiar with opera are surprised to see familiar arias sung by performers in inappropriate costumes, accompanied by irrelevant music, against a mise-en-scène that, in Thoreau's phrase, marches to a different drummer. Those less sympathetic to the culture of opera find the work only tweaking their distaste.

The performers go about their business oblivious to the audience. By asking the nineteen singers to select their favorite arias, Cage could trust them to perform professionally what they have done before (and could perhaps do in their sleep), in spite of unusual distractions. Thanks to the Cagean principle of autonomous parts, such arias become not representational but abstract. Any opera lover trying to play the pedantic game of identifying allusions will soon be defeated by the abundance of them.

What must be seen to be believed is the degree of discontinuity. The background flats move up and down, in and out, seemingly at their own whim, making a show on their own; some images are tilted. Though several arias are sung simultaneously, the singers rarely acknowledge one another. Bouncing around the stage is another set of performers, some in leotards, others informally dressed, who go about their bits only occasionally aware of the singers. The stage lights point in all directions and change autonomously, sometimes leaving soloists in darkness. The theater's back wall is visible throughout, becoming a backdrop so neutral that anything can happen in front of it. In the pit are musicians whose platform occasionally rises to that of the stage before descending again. One recurring theme is incongruity raised to a higher level, with gags that survive repeated hearing. Especially in *Europera 1* there was nearly continuous giggling in the audience.

Some of the individual moves have an obvious charm. A woman suspends a fishing pole into the orchestra pit; before long, she pulls out a cloth fish nearly half her size. An aria is sung by an alto who is seated on a plate that is dragged along the floor. As her saucer approaches a bathtub, she climbs into it, continuing her aria. In another bit, a baritone sings his aria while two dancers paint his arms. Near the end of *Europera 1*, a female head emerges from a hole in the floor, her voice in song. It was a special pleasure to see nineteen performers emerge in continually new guises. The crowning theatrical touch was a zeppelin that flew out into the audience, distracting attention upward while the stage action continued; every opera henceforth needs at least one flying object, I decided.

At SUNY-Purchase, *Europera* was performed in a big theater that had a curtain that went up; the performers sounded and looked like opera singers; the musicians in the orchestra pit looked and sounded like professionals. It is an opera that begs to belong to the operatic canon. (Because the performance of arias amid distractions depends upon the competence of professionals, I doubt if amateurs could do it half as well.) What is missing from *Europera* is narrative, which is to say the thread connecting one incident (or aria) to another. The question implicit here is whether operatic musical theater can succeed without narrative; I think it can.

Europera 2 differed from *1* in being denser and faster. Half the length of the first part, it seemed to have an equal amount of action, this time performed by a fresh cast. Whereas no more than four arias were sung at any one time in *Europera 1*, in *2* I counted as many as seven going on simultaneously. The scene changes so fast, so continually, that someone glancing at his program, say, could raise his or her eyes to a different world. Nothing lasts too long (except, to some, the thing itself).

Even on third viewing, I found myself discovering details that I'd missed before (e.g., real water dropping from a dark cloud).

The falsest moves in the opening performance came from the bass Heinz Hagenau, who, once he donned a kilt and brandished a sword, began mugging to the audience. Later some of the dancers showed off their virtuosic suppleness, drawing attention to themselves by means that were contextually inappropriate. What must be understood is that, all gossip to the contrary notwithstanding, Cage was not finally an apostle of wayward freedom, or "anything goes"; he was really devoted to disciplined constraints that must be observed. One rule is that individual performers cannot do egotistical gestures. It would have been similarly false for a singer to move intentionally his or her body into a spotlight.

Elsewhere I have suggested that Cage's bigger works tend to be better than his smaller pieces; and by its abundance of materials, *Europera* begs to be compared with his other big pieces such as *Roaratorio* and *HPSCHD*, whose premiere was in a sixteen-thousand-seat basketball arena at the University of Illinois. To my mind, as a veteran Cage-watcher, *Europera* pales beside the latter, which was really an unfettered exploration of alternative performance in a profoundly alternative theatrical space. For instance, by having more seats than spectators, *HPSCHD* allowed the audience to move around, in contrast to the experience of being imprisoned in the long rows at Purchase.

Whereas *HPSCHD* was a vision of peaceful chaos, ordered disorder, likewise without any conductor, *Europera* is essentially a reinterpretation of opera, with operatic materials, performed within the context of opera. Remember that appropriating European music, at once irreverently but respectfully, is an old American tradition, exemplified by Charles Ives, Louis Armstrong, and many others; but only Cage would make a work consisting *wholly* of quotations and yet, in its rigorously uninflected discontinuous structure, possessing his unique artistic signature.

The political achievement of Cage's art, here and elsewhere, is the elimination of hierarchy. Just as no note is more important than any other, so no quotation is honored above the others and no singer is featured over the others. Onstage the dancers have a presence equal to the singers; and when a stagehand becomes visible, he or she looks like one of the performers. When members of the company take their bows, there is no conductor to lead them. By third viewing, what seemed innovative at first had become classic, quite classic.

The question has been raised of whether *Europera* could succeed on disc. I was reminded of the 1969 Nonesuch recording of *HPSCHD* that, while only a partial representation of that piece's original performance, has nonetheless survived as an interesting record, the epitome of sustained chaotic sound. (I remember Aaron Copland, hosting a radio series in the 1970s, dismissing it as beyond the bounds of music.) While I might like to have a record or compact disc of *Europera*, what I would most of all prefer would be a videotape, preferably for a large-screen projection TV. Because productions are likely to differ from one another to degrees greater than normal in an opera's life, what would be better yet is a set of videocassettes, each from a different venue, so that I could enjoy Frankfurt on one night, Purchase on another, somewhere else on a third, and so forth.

One innovative opera merits support for another. It seems that, having established himself as a credible opera composer, Cage was asked to propose a sequel he would call "Nohopera," lexically combining Japanese Noh with European opera. As he explained, "Its subtitle would be 'Or the Complete Musical Works of Marcel Duchamp.' It would take another two to four years." That is to say, it could have become his abundant masterpiece for the nineties (and his eighties). Perhaps someone else will do it.

We tend to think of avant-garde artists as flashy adventurers who enter new territory before retreating or retiring into more conventional work; but perhaps the most extraordinary thing about Cage was that into his seventies he continued to be audacious and original. What the Frankfurt commission for *Europera* offered him was an opportunity to open up a genre commonly regarded as stagnant, rewarding us with pleasant surprises and incidentally creating an opera worth seeing, in my experience, again and again.

• *I–VI* (1988–1989)

When those powers-that-be behind selecting the 1988–1989 Charles Eliot Norton Professor at Harvard chose John Cage, they knew in advance that he would not pontificate in the manner of previous holders of that revolving chair (Ben Shahn for *The Shape of Content*, Igor Stravinsky for *Poetics of Music*, etc.). They also knew that Cage, unlike certain previous Nortons, would write his own stuff, which, furthermore, would not resemble traditional exposition but be a kind of poetry. Thankfully, there was enough respect for Cage to produce a handsome book of these lectures twelve inches high, well over one-inch thick, with two audiocassette tapes on an accompanying card, all moderately priced by current standards.

I–VI, as the package is modestly called, actually has two texts. The first is Cage's six lectern-based recitations. This dominates most of 420 pages. The second part is a transcript of his informal seminars, given in response to his generous assumption that, since the main presentations were difficult, he should make himself available to respond to questions. This prose runs continuously along the bottom of each page, as a kind of smaller-type counterpoint that is four lines high and six and a half inches wide, with the unidentified questioners speaking in an italic typeface and Cage answering in Roman in this book. Further to create the illusion of a continuous conversation, the transcripts are printed wholly without commas, periods, capitalizations, or breaks for new paragraphs.

One quality I find in this part of *I–IV*, as nowhere else in print, is Cage's rare ability to respond intelligently to interrogations that most of us would find unintelligible. I remember being on a panel with him in 1977, one Saturday afternoon in a SoHo art gallery. From the audience came questions that made Merce Cunningham, Nam June Paik, Dore Ashton, and myself look at one another in puzzlement. Without hesitation,

Cage took the microphone, looked directly at the questioner, and delivered a coherent reply that made those beside him collapse in awe. Some moments in this counterpoint reminded me of that exquisite performance.

Cage initially produced poetic texts that, by operations mixing choice and chance, drew selectively upon prior texts. (He spoke of his results as "poetry," as do I, because they cannot be classified anywhere else.) For *Empty Words* he chose Thoreau's remarks about acoustic experience (including music). Cage's next poetic sequence went through James Joyce's *Finnegans Wake*, producing five different texts composed entirely of Joyce's words. For these last poems he developed the form he still favors, the mesostic. Whereas an acrostic is composed horizontally from a key word extending down the left margin, a mesostic situates the axis word in the middle. He spoke of his results as "poetry" because they cannot be classified anywhere else.

For his first departure from Joyce, the chapbook *Composition in Retrospect* (Westdeutscher Rundfunk, 1982), Cage selected ten words important to his esthetic experience: method, structure, intention, discipline, notation, indeterminacy, interpenetration, imitation, devotion, circumstances; but instead of drawing upon texts written by others, this time he horizontally wrote words out of his own mind (much as he did with "Diary," his major poem of the late 1960s, which was written within different constraints). *Composition in Retrospect*, his most satisfactory middle-length poetic text, is also the closest semblance of an intellectual autobiography that he has written so far.

For his Norton lectures, Cage continued writing mesostics; but to the earlier collection of ten key words he has added five more: variable structure, nonunderstanding, contingency, inconsistency, performance. Instead of writing out of his own head (or drawing upon a single literary source), here he selected words from several disparate sources: Ludwig Wittgenstein,

Marshall McLuhan, Buckminster Fuller's followers, daily newspapers during the summer of 1988, his own *Composition in Retrospect* (curiously), among others. The result is a more expansive text that not only befits Cage's taste for heady ideas but encompasses the whole world, in part because it draws upon writings with global range, its theme becoming meditations on a scale at once personal and sociopolitical. Because its effects are so drawn out, a short quotation might be less sufficient than usual; nonetheless, consider this:

> space vehIcle earth
> to work with it in the Most long term humanly advantageous ways
> whIch as
> copper and aluminum and sTeel
> we chose to keep efficiency levels And
> developmenT how can we accelerate
> earth's present economIc and industrial
> prOblems of thermal
> uNdeveloped nature
> as those used In
> costuMes
> In
> The
> All
> in The
> sIdes
> Of
> aNd

By opening out and encompassing all at a considerable length, *I–VI* comes to resemble, more than any other American poem, Walt Whitman's "Song of Myself." Need I say that, very much like *Finnegans Wake*, Cage's *I–VI* is at once unreadable and *re*readable. The tape of the fourth lecture helps, especially if heard with the text in hand; listen to it as you would a piece of music, for among its themes is the possibility of less-syntactic verbal communication.

Just as his *Europera* (1987) ranks among his best music theater—indeed, among the most innovative music theater anyone has done in the past few decades—so *I–VI* is his finest poem, a major poem in a unique style, surely among the best American epic poems of the post-WWII period, although the poetry czars would be the last to acknowledge it.

• Roaratorio (1989): John Cage as a Radio Artist

While Cage's music has always been known and his writing became known, his radio art remains almost unknown. Mostly produced for German stations, the bulk of it is not yet available through public channels. My assumption is that eventually Cage's extraordinary audio art will become more familiar, if not through radio broadcasts then at least through discs.

Radio has so receded from cultural view that we can rarely speak of any broadcast as a "cultural event," but that epithet was an accurate description for the first New York City broadcast of the complete version of John Cage's *Roaratorio*. Begun over a decade ago as a commission for West German radio, *Roaratorio* has been broadcast over public stations around the world; it also became the score for a superlative Merce Cunningham choreography. However, only parts of it were broadcast on radio here before.

The work began in 1978 with Klaus Schöning's invitation to Cage to read aloud one of his *Writings Through Finnegans Wake*. These are a series of Cagean texts in which Cage extracts sequentially certain words from Joyce's classic and then sets them on mesostic axes composed of the name "James Joyce." In *Writing for the Second Time Through Finnegans Wake*, which he chose to read for Westdeutscher Rundfunk, the opening is:

> wroth with twone nathandJoe
> A
> Malt
> jhEm
> Shen

pftJschute
sOlid man
that the humptYhillhead of humself
is at the knoCk out
in thE park

Asked to add a "musical background" to this declamation, Cage decided to gather sounds recorded in every geographic place mentioned in Joyce's text. For guidance he
consulted Louis Mink's book, *A Finnegans Wake Gazetteer*. By
birth a prodigious correspondent, Cage wrote friends around
the world and asked Schöning to do likewise; but since most of
Joyce's places were in Ireland, he decided to spend a whole
month there himself with the American audio consultant John
David Fullemann, recording not only places but native musics.
All these field recordings were then gathered at IRCAM in Paris,
where Cage and Fullemann spent a month assembling them by
chance operations onto sixteen-track tape machines, making
spectacularly dense acoustic mixes, at once cacophonous and
euphonious, that, while they may vary in detail, are roughly
similar in quality (and quantity) for the entire duration.

Whereas some Cage pieces have contained much less
sound than music used to have, others have contained much
more; for Cage was at different times a prophet of both minimalism in art and abundance. *Roaratorio* falls securely into the
second tradition. The continuous bass, or cantus firmus, if you
will, is the sound of Cage himself reading. On top of that is an
abundant mix of sounds in which the most sustained presence
is Irish folk music. In that last respect, *Roaratorio* structurally
resembles *HPSCHD* (1969), which has always stood for me as
the earlier masterpiece of Cagean abundance. In *HPSCHD*,
beneath the continuous microtonal din, is the sound of seven
harpsichords playing selections from Mozart to the present; in
the single available recording these harpsichords tend to stand

out from the mix to much the same degree that Irish music does in the new piece. To my taste, *Roaratorio* is as significant as *HPSCHD*; indeed, as a masterpiece on a masterpiece it ranks among Cage's very best works.

Given the low interest in exploratory acoustic art in American radio, "public" as well as private, it is no surprise that Cage produced *Roaratorio* in Europe, initially for Westdeutscher Rundfunk in Cologne, where these radio works are produced not by WDR's music department, which nonetheless airs transcriptions of Cage's music, but by *Hörspiel*, pronounced "heur-speel," which translates literally as "ear-play" and is, in the German radio bureaucracies, a production department distinct from literature and features.

The word *Hörspiel* traditionally meant radio plays, which were customarily not soap operas or situation comedies (familiar to American radio) but something else—poetic texts, indefinite enough to stimulate the listener's imagination, whose words are read by well-cultivated voices, recorded in a studio, abetted by minimal sound effects. In American radio the closest analogue was Archibald MacLeish's *Fall of the City* (1938); perhaps the most famous English-language radio play of this kind is Dylan Thomas's *Under Milk Wood* (1953). Since *Hörspiel* as a word is far more graceful and encompassing than any English equivalent, I will henceforth use it without italics or umlaut, as though it were an English word.

Two cultural products that Germans value far more than we are opera and horspiel. For the latter there are annual prizes, the most prestigious being the Hörspielpreis der Kriegsblinden (or war-blind); for more experimental endeavors there is the Karl-Sczuka-Preis, which was awarded to *Roaratorio* back in 1979. Horspiels are also collected into textbooks that are taught in the universities and high schools. Anthologies and critical books are frequently published; current critical issues are discussed at annual conferences. There is even a prodigious encyclopedia, now outdated, with the unfortunate title of *Hörspielführer*. Twice a year the horspiel department of Westdeutscher Rundfunk issues a book-length catalogue of forthcoming productions, most of which are displayed on an eight-by-eight-inch page. In each of these WDR books is such an abundance of radio art that showing a recent volume to an American radio professional is to watch him or her faint dead away.

Within the past two decades a producer on WDR's permanent staff, Klaus Schöning developed a distinct alternative to traditional German horspiel. Where radio plays had previously defined an intermedium between literature and theater, Schöning gravitated to points between literature and music. Coupled to this taste was an ambition for sponsoring classics—works that could be rebroadcast year after year, not only in Germany but around the world. Indicatively, the surest measure of his success, especially in his colleagues' eyes, is not how many listeners he has but how many horspiel prizes his artists have won.

Even though Schöning did not enter Cage's life until 1978, the latter had an earlier creative interest in radio and its principal storage medium of audiotape. His *Imaginary Landscape No. 1* (1939) was written, to quote his publisher's catalog, for "two variable-speed phono-turntables, frequency recordings, muted piano and cymbal; to be performed as a recording or broadcast." Two details perhaps unfamiliar to us now are that these "frequency records" had either sustained tones or sliding tones that were, supposedly, scientifically generated, and that the speeds of those old-time record turntables could be varied by hand. In Cage's mind when he wrote this piece were certain unprecedented acoustic capabilities available in radio studios (that were new at the time).

A few years later Cage was commissioned to produce "music" for Kenneth Patchen's radio play, *The City Wears a Slouch Hat*; what he wanted to do here likewise presaged *Roaratorio*: "Take the sounds out of the play, and make the music out of those sounds." Several years after that he premiered *Imaginary Landscape No. 4* (1951), for twelve radios and twenty-four performers, one manning the volume control of each machine and another changing the stations, in response to Cage's scored instructions.

The second strand behind Cage's radio art was his early interest in audiotape, which is so familiar to us now we tend to forget that it became commonly available only after World War II. Prior to that, sound was recorded on continuous wire that, while it could be cut, could not be spliced easily; that is, its parts could not be reassembled without making thunderous telltale sounds. Precisely because acoustic tape, by contrast, could be spliced gracefully, sounds separately recorded could be fused together without distracting interruptions.

Cage remembered that when the French composer Pierre Schaeffer first introduced him to audiotape in 1948, he rejected its possibilities; within a few years, though, he was working on *Williams Mix* (1952). For this maximal work he gathered taped sounds from a universe of sources; these tapes were cut into small pieces, some much shorter than audiotape is wide, and then spliced together into an aural pastiche that is continually leaping, with unprecedented shifts, from one kind of sound (and one acoustic space) to another. To complicate the audio experience of *Williams Mix* yet further, Cage required that eight separate tapes be made, and then that in live concerts any or all of them could be played simultaneously.

In the wake of *Roaratorio*'s success, Cage produced other radio works for Schöning and WDR. His next major piece, *Ein Alphabet* (1982), also began with a text that (unlike before) was translated into German. Most of "James Joyce, Erik Satie, Marcel Duchamp: An Alphabet" consists of mesostics that Cage wrote out of his own head on the names of these three heroes, all of whom, in Cage's curious judgment, have made works that "resisted the march of understanding and so are as fresh now as when they first were made." Interspersed among the mesostics are long passages from the writings of each of these men. (The whole original English text appears, along with Cage's spikey preface, in his collection of writings, X [1983, 1986].)

The WDR production of _Ein Alphabet_ honors the conventions of traditional radio theater, in that certain roles were assigned to various performers: the French musicologist Daniel Charles reading Satie (in inept German), the American artist George Brecht representing Duchamp (in better German), Cage himself reading Joyce (in the original neologistic superEnglish). As the narrative passes through various scenes, their settings are occasionally reinforced with sound effects that tend to be very abrupt, usually sketching a scene suggestively (rather than filling it in). As other figures are included, their voices are represented by yet other performers speaking German—Dick Higgins as Robert Rauschenberg, Christian Wolff as Henry David Thoreau, Buckminister Fuller as himself, etc.

Ein Alphabet reflects the arrival of audiotape in that it was composed from many parts that were separately recorded (in fact, on two continents, at different times). Insofar as I can understand German, I think the work very good, filled as it is with interesting departures within the tradition of radio plays as well as suggestive moves that others can adopt (not the least of which is the imaginary conversation among historic figures who did not know each other). On the other hand, Cage himself disliked all the leaps from scene to scene. "All those scenes," he once told me, "have beginnings and ends. That's what annoys me." In my interpretation this caveat means that _Ein Alphabet_ lacks the continuous, uninflected, nonclimactic structure that, in _Roaratorio_ as well as his work in other media, has been the signature of Cage's art.

Muoyce (1983) is a more familiar Cagean performance— essentially a solo reading of his _Writing for the Fifth Time Through Finnegans Wake_; but to complicate the largely uninflected declamation, Cage decided to use a multitrack audiotape device he had used before (mostly in live performance). The first of the piece's four parts has him whispering the same text simultaneously four times all the way through, in a nonsynchronous chorus; the second part is a self-trio; the third part, a duet; the fourth (and shortest) part, a solo. He interrupts his whispering for full-voiced speaking only when the original text had italics. Here, as well in the previous work that resembles it, *Empty Words* (1974–1975), I have personally come to find this minimalism less substantial. Always true to his principles, Cage said, "I find this one easier [than *Ein Alphabet*]. What makes this easy for me is that the quiet sober mind is assumed and is not disturbed, even by the lightning imitations which come though the loud interrupting sounds, because they don't really interrupt. Once they are gone, the whispering continues."

HMCIEX (or *HCE-mix*, with its letters alternating) was commissioned by both WDR and International Composers in Los Angeles, which benefited from the Olympics fallout. Though *HMCIEX* [1984] is a dense mix, it is also a simple piece (that, contrary to Cage's esthetics, does not resist understanding). In honor of the Olympics, it is an international pastiche of folk songs (and in that respect reminiscent of Karlheinz Stockhausen's similarly ecumenical *Hymnen* [1979]; but whereas Stockhausen favored Western sources, Cage draws more upon the Third World). One quality that separates *HMCIEX* from Cage's earlier mixes is that its sources are longer and thus more often identifiable upon first hearing. A second problem is that, given such long excerpts, the sound often falls into a regular beat that is utterly contrary to Cage's esthetics. Compared to *Roaratorio*, *HMCIEX* is a slighter work, that is charming nonetheless.

What Cage did in his radio art is define other possibilities for presenting recorded sound, and thus other ways of making records. When Cage has been criticized for releasing records that were "not as good" as live performances of his work, the reply was that, aside from *Williams Mix*, his music has not been written for tape. Now, given the demands of modern radio, he composed for tape, exploiting its unique capabilities, to make works that are true both to tape and to his esthetics. In my opinion he produced, at least in *Roaratorio*, a transcription as good as any of his earlier records.

In this last respect Cage discovered in radio a truth that another adventurous North American musician also made sometime before him—the Canadian pianist Glenn Gould. Frustrated as a composer, unwilling to do live performances, Gould in Toronto made a series of radio features, scarcely heard here, that represent to my mind the best radio art ever produced in North America. With multitrack audiotape, Gould could mix speech with speech, speech with music, and music with music, not only in ways that, given his materials, would be impossible in live performance, but in fugal arrangements that would also be beautiful. In other words, invitations from radio stations forced both these verbal musicians to compose for tape as they had not composed before, producing valuable work that, if not for these radio invitations, probably would not have otherwise happened.

Part III. The Legacy

• method • structure • intention • discipline • notation •

indeterminacy • interpenetration • imitation • devotion •
• **method** • **structure**
circumstances • method • structure • intention • discipline
• **intention** • **discipline**
notation • indeterminacy • interpenetration • imitation •

devotion • circumstances • method • structure • intention•
• **notation**

discipline • notation • indeterminacy • interpenetration • imita
• **indeterminacy**
• devotion • circumstances • method • structure • intention •

• **interpenetration**
discipline • notation • indeterminacy • interpenetration •

imitation • devotion • circumstances • method • structure
• **initiation**

intention • discipline • notation • indeterminacy •
• **devotion**

interpenetration • imitation • devotion • circumstances • met
• **circumstances**
• structure • intention• discipline • notation • indeterminacy •

interpenetration • imitation • devotion • circumstances • met

• Rolyholyover: Antiseptic Havoc in the Name of John Cage

Rolyholyover began as a posthumous exhibition devoted to John Cage, purportedly with his imprimatur, at the Los Angeles Museum of Contemporary Art in late 1993. It toured subsequently to Houston and New York's Guggenheim Museum, where I finally saw it; it also went to museums in Japan and Philadelphia. To say that it had serious problems is to underestimate the degree of sabotage not only of Cage himself but of his unique esthetics.

Problems began with the exhibition's subtitle, "A Circus." The image of a circus frequently appears in Cage's talk as an esthetic model of multicentered, nonhierarchic kinetic activity. He was thinking not of the European-style circus, which takes place in a single circular performance space, but the American three-ring circus, traditionally associated with the name of Ringling, where spectators are continually distracted by activities at the sides of their attention (and thus nudge one another to look elsewhere). In my *John Cage* (1970, 1991) is his recollection of his piece *Musicircus* (November 17, 1967), in which dancers, musicians, mimes, and even spectators were performing separately and simultaneously. There were:

> "the composer Salvatore Martirano, who, like the others, used a group of performers and gave a program of his own; Jocy de Oliveira (Carvalho), who gave a piano recital that included Ben Johnston's *Knocking Piece*, music by Morton Feldman, etc.; Lejaren Hiller; Herbert Brün; James Cuomo and his band; another jazz band; David Tudor and Gordon Mumma; Norma Marder giving a voice recital, sometimes accompanying a dancer, Ruth Emerson; the mime Claude Kipnis, who responded with a whole sound environment; perhaps

others I don't remember. In the center of the floor was
a metallic construction upon which the audience could
make sounds. No directions were given anyone."

Two years later Cage staged *HPSCHD* (1969), which I regard
as the masterpiece of Cagean performance and which I experienced as a circus.

Because of administrative misinformation, I had tickets to
attend the Ringling Circus the same night as the Guggenheim
opening and thus went directly from the latter to Madison
Square Garden. The first criticism to make is that *Rolyholyover*
wasn't much of a circus—neither by American standards nor
Cagean standards. (Indeed, on opening night, which included
both Cage's friends and a large contingent from AT&T, an
exhibition benefactor, the SoHo Guggenheim resembled a zoo.)
With four static exhibition spaces separated by floor-to-ceiling
walls, *Rolyholyover* was essentially no different from any other multimedia show. In one room were paintings, a second had
books and posters, a third had drawings, and a fourth displayed either slides or videos on a single screen. Two departures were that the paintings were mounted at various heights
and that their arrangement was reportedly changed from day
to day.

The catalog quotes Cage as wishing that "the exhibition
would change so much that if you came back a second day you
wouldn't recognize it." While the first move could be appreciated by most spectators, the second required him or her to
return the following day and was thus available only to a few.
Those who returned, as I did, would have discovered that this
claim too was not only false but esthetically problematic, as the
exhibition looked pretty much the same from day to day—
indeed, scarcely different at the end of its three-month stay as it
did at the beginning. What daily redistribution really represents
is a *symbol* of kineticism—a symbol that must be imaginative-
ly interpreted (with some curatorial coaching) for its ulterior

meaning to be derived; but nothing in art was more anathema to Cage and Cagean esthetics than symbolism.

Calling the exhibition a circus thus became a pretension that permeated everything else, which is to say that *Rolyholyover* was not what was claimed for it. The catalog came as a box, in which a variety of miscellaneous documents were reproduced. About the critical essays the less said the better. One simply recycles sentiments that might have been striking and courageous in 1970 but are by now embarrassingly familiar; to say it is utterly devoid of original insight is to be generous. Another essay, drawn from a doctorate, is so clumsily written, with sentences tacked onto one another in unconsidered ways, that I doubt if anyone finished reading it. (More than one Cage fanatic told me that he failed it, or it him.) A third is derivative to a degree Cage, who despised derivativeness, would have found embarrassing. A fourth is self-consciously impenetrable. (Be flattered, John—only about *major* artists is so much bad writing published in museum catalogs.) My own name appears in the catalogue listed among "artists in the exhibition," though none of my art appears—not even the nonsyntactic prose of *Recyclings*, which was explicitly dedicated to Cage and realized as both a videotape (1975) and a book (1974, 1984). Need I wager dollars to donuts that others on this "artists" list were similarly absent from the show? It is hard to imagine a commercial publisher distributing this problematic book unless it were given gratis—fully paid for by the sponsoring institutions.

What this exhibition indicates, along with some recent conferences based on his name, is that Cage has become the province of second-rate minds who have not thought much about the subject (which requires considerable thinking, in part because his activities were so original). Just after Cage's death, Kyle Gann, the *Village Voice*'s music critic, berated ignorant obituary writers, overnight experts, particularly at *The New York Times*, citing instead some "real Cage scholars."

Indicatively, none of Gann's experts were involved with this, which made a point of featuring opportunistic beginners who were, alas, this time none too lucky.

Another claim made for this exhibition is that it realized Cage's plans. It is unfortunate that he's no longer around to approve or disapprove. One problem in dealing with Cage himself is that while he talked about "chance," he also practiced constraint. That is to say that for his poetry he chose *Finnegans Wake* rather than another text; for *HPSCHD* he chose a large basketball arena, an abundance of slides and films, and tapes of music in fifty-two different scales. Once those initial major decisions were made, minor details could be left to chance. What *Rolyholyover* introduced to the exhibition space was the daily chance rearrangement of the available materials, which at the Guggenheim at least is finally trivial; what's missing is the kind of inventive constraint that, say, continuously moving walls would have provided. If only because I've been around long enough, this exhibition reminded me of certain 1960s Cagean composers who assimilated the message about chance but missed the secret of a crucial constraint. Their works at their time (now as forgotten as their names) tended to be messy agglomerations.

Because the materials of *Rolyholyover* were so disparate (and mounted at different heights), the rooms resembled a junk shop, in this case with well-scrubbed walls and floors (which is to say a junk shop out of its original context); the impression was essentially comic, if not by intention at least by default. In the largest room were paintings drawn from a variety of sources, tagged only by numbers (for which one needed to consult a spiral-bound guidebook), a few of which were from artists less familiar than the others (who were thus hurt by the lack of immediate identification). In another room were cabinets with books distributed one to a drawer. On a table were Cage's books from Wesleyan University Press, which on my visits were all untouched, perhaps because it is commonly known that they do not succeed at the fundamental bookish job of making Cage's writing and thought more generally accessible.

Beside the cabinets was a video monitor playing, when I was there, Ernie Kovacs kinescopes, which have nothing to do with Cage (and which I doubt if he saw, because he didn't have a television while Kovacs was alive and didn't much watch television after he got one). In one of the drawers I found Marjorie Perloff's *The Futurist Moment* (1986), which has only a few more references to Cage than a 1960 Manhattan telephone directory; in drawer No. 46 was my own anthology *Breakthrough Fictioneers* (1973), which has no Cage at all. (No, nobody was paid off.) You would look in vain for two major Cage books (which were also absent from the curatorial list sent to me): *Writings Through Finnegans Wake* (1978) and *Writing Through Finnegans Wake* (1978), which are not identical, though you can imagine how slight differences in spelling might confuse a thick curator. The exhibition likewise neglects Sorel Etrog's *About Roaratorio* (1982), a typographically spectacular "artist's book," even though its author (b. 1933) is a prominent Rumanian-Canadian painter. In this room too was a 1993 photograph by a much-touted emerging black artist, Lorna Simpson, which Cage surely did not see because he died in 1992. Undercurated in most respects, *Rolyholyover* suffered from overcuration in others.

A third room contained only Cage's visual art, which here consisted mostly of pointless abstractions in various colors, sizes, and shapes. Distributed at various heights, none stood out from the others—they did not gain from accompanying one another. Here were also a few samples of his exquisitely calligraphed black-and-white scores. The first time I visited this room, accompanied by a Cage assistant from a quarter-century ago, I asked her which work she liked best. She chose the most elaborate score, a "Table of Preparations," as did I, even though it was mounted at the level of our knees, because it has a much stronger visual identity than the self-consciously arty abstractions. What was missing from this room, whose contents did not change, was Cage's best visual art—the Plexiglas panels for Marcel Duchamp produced in 1969 and the accompanying very dark silk-screened prints. What was also inexplicably missing from display was the intrinsically richest Cagean score, *The Song Books* (1970), its absence illustrating the truth that a curatorial commitment to "chance" does not necessarily bring critical research skills.

The great misfortune, not just for this exhibition, is that Cage is no longer alive. I wonder what he would have thought of this mess that was neither cunningly ordered nor purposefully purposeless; my hunch is that he surely would have gently, but firmly, recommended changes before it went on the road, rightly fearing this would undermine possible further exhibitions of his work. It is hard to believe, for instance, he would have accepted the academic division of his art into four separate spaces and, for another, he would have wanted both his very best visual art and his *Finnegans Wake* books to be absent. One of his intellectual virtues was a refusal to make claims that couldn't be verified—"A Circus" this never would be for him. Though Cage could seem casual, he was not intellectually opportunistic and certainly not as self-defeating as he was portrayed here. Unless someone is unseemly stupid, the implicit theme of this show was diminishing not only Cage but the institutions sponsoring it. Much like that awful 1960s post-Cagean music, it publicly established how much havoc can be done in his name in his absence, less by enemies than by unastute purported friends.

• Homosexuality

Everyone who knew John Cage thought him gay; the suspicion of homosexuality probably crossed the mind of nearly everyone hearing his peculiar voice. Nonetheless, mention of it rarely, if ever, appeared in print within his lifetime. The first citation I can recall is in David Revill's biography, The Roaring Silence (1992), which appeared just after Cage's death. (Even there the information is attributed to someone else speaking at a conference rather than asserted in the author's own voice.) In an era in which many homosexual celebrities "came out" or were "outed," it seems to me remarkable that identification of Cage's sexuality was so rarely made public.

In retrospect I realize that he worked at keeping it secret. Most of his biographies acknowledge his marriage to Xenia Kashevaroff in the late 1930s, even though it ended in divorce less than a decade later. A composer friend of Cage's from the 1950s once told me the story of him and his wife playing Scrabble with Cage and his parents at the latter's home on the Upper East Side in the 1950s. Mother Cage, who was no dummy, turned to the younger composer's wife and said, "Don't you think John should marry again?" That suggests to me that the first people kept in the dark were his parents.

Indeed, on the afternoon of May 14, 1992, just three months before his death, Cage interrupted my telephone conversation with his assistant Andrew Culver to ask that I delete "with love" from the dedication of John Cage, Writer (1993). It now reads: "From both JC & RK / To Lou Harrison." When I drafted that dedication, I knew that Cage and Harrison had been close, more than a half-century before, and that there was still enough affection between them for Cage to attend Harrison's New York concerts late in 1990. Surprised by Cage's request for the deletion, I nonetheless honored it even after his death.

Given this background, I was shocked to find the longest chapter of *Composed in America* (1994, University of Chicago Press, ed. by Marjorie Perloff and Charles Junkerman) quoting Cage's revelations of his homosexual activities during his "Los Angeles Years, 1912–1938." The article's author is Thomas S. Hines, a UCLA architecture professor, whose footnotes say he obtained the testimony in a "five-hour interview, most of which was taped, [that] took place in Cage's apartment over two days," which were May 21 and 23, 1992.

Were this interview made at another place, at another time, it would be more credible to me. However, since it was made in the same home where he had a week before spoken to me, I don't accept it. Quite simply, to acknowledge Hines's authority you would need to believe that Cage would admit in one week the kind of love he preferred to deny the week before. My suspicion, knowing nothing, is that Hines is attributing to Cage, now dead, information and anecdotes that, if true (they might be), were obtained from other sources. (There are some other recurring deleterious inventions in the Perloff-Junkerman anthology that disqualify it from any canon of Cage criticism.)

While homosexual connections and sympathy were surely important to many composers of Cage's generation, it didn't take me long to discover, when I first examined the connections between sexuality and style three decades ago, that they weren't important to Cage and his group (few of whom were gay). His closest gay colleagues worked in areas other than music. In contrast to certain homosexual tonal composers, Cage was not promiscuous; he did not exploit sex to advance his career or to promise career advancement to others. Indeed, if he were seeing anyone other than his lifetime companion Merce Cunningham during the quarter century I knew him, I could not identify that third person and did not hear anybody else identify a third person. Perhaps those who knew the truth were honoring the wish mentioned at the beginning of this essay. In that respect, the most truthful line in Hines's memoir (even though it may not be true) has Cage saying, "Once I'm doing something serious, I do not think about sex." That's another way of saying that sex wasn't important in Cage's art and thought.

• I Saw John Cage at the Millrose Games

Perhaps the greatest index of the influence of John Cage is that he made me appreciate certain ways of the world in Cagean ways. For many fans of competitive running and jumping, the annual Millrose Games is the apex of the New York City indoor-track season; for me it is the epitome of nonhierarchic, noncentered Cagean performance. The floor of Madison Square Garden, essentially a basketball court and hockey rink some sixty yards by twenty, is covered with a four-lane wooden track that runs circularly along the edge and is drastically sloped ("banked") at its narrow ends (to compensate for a sharp turn-to-reversal). Whereas the standard outdoor circular track has 440 yards, requiring four laps to a mile, this one is approximately 150 yards long, requiring eleven laps to the mile. Inside the track is paraphernalia for the pole vault, the high jump, and the long jump, as well as another straightaway track for the sixty-yard dashes and hurdles. The events in 1995 began promptly at 5:45 P.M. with a series of relays and continued past 10:30 P.M., with no clear break in the activities for roughly five continuous hours. Five hours was incidentally the length of Cage's greatest theatrical creation, *HPSCHD* (1969), which likewise took place in an indoor sports arena (Assembly Hall at the University of Illinois).

What first of all marks the Millrose Games as Cagean performance is that two and often three events occur simultaneously. While runners are going around the main track, pole vaulters and jumpers are flinging themselves to various heights and distances. This means that spectators must constantly choose where to look. More than once I heard some members of the audience cheering something that had completely escaped my attention. Curiously, the announcer describing the running is not the same man identifying the pole vaulters, which means that the voices sometimes interrupt each other. More than once I saw a pole vaulter in midair, about to execute his concluding moves over the crossbar just as the starter's gun resounded coincidentally. In its diffusion of spectator attention, the Millrose Games resembles the traditional American three-ring circus, which incidentally also takes place in Madison Square Garden later in the spring; such a circus was always an esthetic ideal for Cage (exploited and compromised though it was by the *Rolyholyover* exhibition, which was subtitled "A Circus," though it scarcely was).

What also makes the Millrose Games Cagean is an abundance of participants coupled to an absence of hierarchy. On the same indoor track were run several sixteen-hundred-meter relays separately for men and women, with each runner doing four hundred meters, within a wide variety of team classifications: local universities, Ivy League universities, public high schools within the five boroughs, suburban high schools, Catholic high schools, local club teams, and "masters" teams (which are limited to runners forty years of age and older). One of the more curious races, Chemical Bank Women's 4 X 400 Meters Indoor Challenge, had the Board of Education team pitted against Memorial Sloan-Kettering, Citibank, IBM, and the FBI. (IBM won, while the FBI finished fifth, apparently amicably. The parallel men's race was won by the Board of Education!)

This is the same track on which some of the meets' stars run—Marcus O'Sullivan in the Wanamaker Mile, Hassiba Boulmerka (an Olympic champion) in the Women's Mile, Reuben Reina in the 3,000 meters, Maria Mutola in the 800 meters, Mark Everett in the 800 meters. Also here, before the same audience, is the High School Boys' solo One-Mile Run, the women's equivalent, a 400-meter race, a 500-meter race,

3,200-meter relays, etc., all of them staged with roughly an equal amount of fanfare. One could identify with the thrill for a young person (or even a master) running on the same boards as a world-class star only a few minutes before or after. (Some barely negotiated the banking, for which they lacked experience; it was both sad and amusing to see amateur runners losing their balance around the turns, while one man fell flat on his stomach, his forward force propelling him up all the way to the track's outer edge.)

I've written elsewhere that the common mark of Cagean masterpieces, as distinct from his lesser pieces, is an *abundance* of unassociated activities. There is no doubt that the Millrose Games by most measures ranks among the most populous sports shows, with so many events within such a small space, and that such an abundance is a key to its esthetic quality. Though the newspapers and the sixty-minute network television program featured only competitions starring celebrities (most of whom did *not* win this year), I found the whole Games superior to any of its parts.

The first time I saw the Millrose Games I sat in expensive seats, perhaps several rows from the edge of the track, but could not see the runners directly in front of me. Essentially the slope of the Garden's seats is designed to make the center stage visible to all, while the space beyond the sidelines of, say, a basketball court can be seen only from seats on the *other* side of the Garden. Since this design hides so much of the track directly below, spectators in front of us began to stand in order to see better, obscuring the entire scene. The surprise this time was that the cheapest seats, at the very top of the house, provided the best view, precisely because the greater slope angle up there enabled one to see more. No one up top ever stood up (except of course to move out of or into his seat). An antisnob anarchist to his guts, Cage would have liked the notion of the cheapest seats being the best.

What I mean to say is that the Millrose Games has John Cage's theatrical signature, even though, in fact, he had nothing to do with it.

Appendix 1
• John Cage Disco-Bibliography

age's antipathy to recordings is well known. He did not own a record player or any cassette players (for either audio or video); he knew nothing about compact discs. Vain in some respects, such as loving to pose for photographers, he apparently did not care about recordings of his own works. He told the story of not wanting to hear the final version of his first long recording, Indeterminacy (1959), where he also performed his work, in this case the reading of prose pieces.

His disinterest in recordings struck me most strongly when I presented him with the typeset of my fresh discography for the 1991 reprint of my 1970 documentary monograph on him. Culled from various sources, it represented the most elaborate listing compiled up to that time; I was proud of it. I had previously shown him proofs of texts involving him, not only because errors bothered him but also because he was an ace proofreader. ("You weren't born in September," he once consoled me, after I apologized for my own insufficiencies.) Not hearing from him about it, while remembering him as efficient about his daily mail, I telephoned a few days later to hear him say, without apology, that he had sent it on to someone else; he had not looked at it at all.

I think one reason for Cage's disinterest in recordings was his own reluctance to confront the question of comparative performance. He knew that a performance of his work could be incorrect, especially when the performers' approach was faulty; but he didn't often say that one reasonably accurate performance was better than any other and I never heard him say any was best. He was not alone in such evasions. No issue poses so many problems even for Cage's most sympathetic critics, such as myself (who has also evaded it). Having no answers, I've consulted my colleagues, even raising the question of evaluating performance at a 1988 university conference devoted to Cage's work. After hearing a lot of palaver, the conference's organizer berated the participants for evading "Richard's serious question." What followed among us then was no better than before.

For instance, there are several available recordings of Cage's earliest extended masterpiece, *The Sonatas and Interludes for Prepared Piano*; among the performers are, in roughly chronological order, Maro Ajemian, Yuji Takahashi, Gerard Fremy, Nada Kolundzija, Joshua Pierce, John Tilbury, and Daryl Rosenberg. I tend to prefer the Ajemian, because it was one I heard first three decades ago and the only one I knew for many years. I once heard a sophisticated New York classical disk jockey recommend it as well for "the quality of the preparations." On second thought, however, neither of those two reasons is sufficient for identifying it as best. Though Cage himself performed the work several times in live concerts, no transcription of his interpretation is known to exist.

What can be recommended is the only available recording of *Williams Mix*, which appears on *The 25-Year Retrospective Concert for the Music of John Cage* (Wergo WEA 0247-2) that brings back into print on two CDs the three LPs that George Avakian privately published more than three decades ago. The classic Cage-Tudor performance of *Indeterminacy* has been reissued as Smithsonian-Folkways CDs (SF 40804-5).

HPSCHD appeared only as a Nonesuch record (H-71224), along with an ingenious instruction sheet for varying the performance on one's home hi-fi console; it hasn't been available for years. Other classic recordings are the Cathy Berberian performance of Cage's *Aria* along with a tape of *Fontana Mix* (Time Records 58003) and Jeanne Kirstein's *Music for Keyboard 1935–1948* (Columbia M2S 819).

The tape of *Roaratorio* appears on both Wergo (WER-6303-2) and Mode (28/29). The former adds to a single CD only 14:14 of Cage alone reading his *Writing for the Second Time Through Finnegans Wake*. The latter, on two CDS, has sixty minutes of Cage reading from the same text and a thirty-one-minute conversation with the work's producer, Klaus Schöning. You pay more money and you get richer background.

Though *Europeras 1* and *2* are unavailable, the scaled-down *Europeras 3* and *4* appear on a Mode CD (38/39). Mode has also issued Irvine Arditti's supremely and sublimely virtuosic recording of Cage's *Freeman Etudes* (32) and the Arditti Quartet's classic disc of Cage's String Quartets (17).

Of the dozens of Cage discs issued since my once-definitive discography, the best I can say is that it is gratifying to see available many Cage pieces that were rarely performed during his lifetime. Nonetheless, too many resemble one another in generating jagged articulations in an atmosphere of silence. Only a few are particularly recommended. Among the purist Cagean performances to come from the Swiss label Hat Hut is *Fifty-eight* (1992) by the Pannonisches Blassorchester (Hat Art CD 6135). Steven Drury is initiating reinterpretations of Cage's piano pieces on several discs from both Crysalis and Mode.

Probably the most accomplished orator of Cage's verbal texts is Eberhard Blum, a Berliner otherwise known as a flutist. His performance of Cage's *Sixty-Two Mesostics re Merce Cunningham* on two CDs (Hat Art 2-6095) is spectacular, his German accent notwithstanding. Blum's declamation of the German translation of Cage's *45' for Speaker* is considerably stronger than Frances-Marie Uitti's needlessly muffled reading of the English text on a companion CD from Hat Art. Her superior recitation of Cage's "Lecture for Nothing," spoken with the enticing accent of an American who has lived for a long time in Europe, appears in her *Works for Cello* (Etcetera KTC2016).

The most ambitious and thus successful recording of Cage's own declamations is "Diary" in a box of eight CDS

(Wergo WER 6231-2 286 231-2), as originally taped at a Swiss radio station. For every change in the original text's typography, the producers altered the acoustic ambiance of Cage's voice. Consider it a masterpiece of spoken-word discs.

What's missing are videotapes of such performance classics as *HPSCHD*, *Roaratorio*, and *Europera*.

Alan Miller produced an informative documentary for NET; Elliott Caplan's film, *Cunningham/Cage*, produced by the Cunningham Foundation itself (463 West Street, New York, NY 10014), and Mitch Corber's videotape, *John Cage: Man and Myth* (1990, 58 East Fourth Street, New York, NY 10003), are both more eccentric and diffuse.

The books that Cage assembled for Wesleyan University Press tend to be collections of short pieces, both expository and experimental, which are by turns accessible and impenetrable, gathered in no particular order and thus usually disappointing to those accustomed to reading a book from beginning to end. Some of my own frustration with them appears in my critical comments in this book. These titles include *Silence* (1961), *A Year from Monday* (1967), *M* (1973), *Empty Words* (1979), and *X* (1983, 1986).

I find more satisfactory the Cage books that began as books, beginning with his *Notations* (Something Else, 1969), which is esthetically the quintessentially Cagean book-art book, but including *Writings About Finnegans Wake* (Printed Editions, 1978) and *I–VI* (Harvard University, 1990). *Mirage Verbal* (Ulysse Fin de Siecle, n.d.) contains mesostics mostly in French based on the writings of Marcel Duchamp. *Composition in Retrospect* (Exact Change, 1993) reprints the most definitive version of the title text, along with *Themes and Variations*, which had appeared as a chapbook several years before. The score of boundless *Song Books* (1970) is available from C. F. Peters, which has other Cage scores (373 Park Avenue South, New York, NY 10016).

Both *John Cage* (ed. Kostelanetz, 1970, rev. 1991) and

John Cage, Writer (ed. Kostelanetz, Limelight, 1993) contain
Cage texts unavailable elsewhere. *Conversing with Cage* (Limelight, 1988) is my composition of passages from interviews that
Cage gave over the years; I could imagine someone else drawing differently from the same well. Many of his performance
texts, as well as his poems, remain scattered to the winds until
they are collected. What is also necessary is a collection of
those fugitive poems that exist only in recipients' letters.

I've tried to collect in *Writings About John Cage* (University of Michigan, 1993) the best extended English-language
criticism that had not previously appeared in books. This
anthology includes several essays by Daniel Charles, the French
critic whom Cage reportedly identified as understanding his
music best. The fullest collection of Charles's writings on Cage
appears not in French or English, the two languages in which
he writes, but in several volumes of German translation from
Merveverlag (Postfach 150 927, D-10671 Berlin, Germany).
Some of the best German-language criticism and documenta-
tion appears in two volumes both edited by Heinz-Klaus Metzger and Rainer Riehn, published successively in 1978 and
1990 by Edition Text + Kritik (Postfach 80 05 29, D-81605
Munich, Germany). Much other Cage criticism is ignorant and
thoughtless to embarrassing degrees.

Appendix II

• ChronoCage

1912	John Cage born September 5, Los Angeles, CA	*Daphnis et Chloe* by Maurice Ravel; Arnold Schoenberg's *Fünf Orchesterstücke* premiered
1913		*Sacre du Printemps* by Stravinsky premiered in Paris; Armory Show held in New York featuring Marcel Duchamp's *Nude Descending a Staircase*
1914–1918		World War I
1916		Henry Cowell introduces tone clusters in *The Banshee*
1919		Merce Cunningham born
1920		Initial demonstration of the Theremin, the first electronic musical instrument; first commercial radio broadcast, featuring musical numbers, made from Detroit; Erik Satie presents the premiere of his *Furniture Music*
1922		First demonstration of Thomas Wilford's Clavilux which projects colors on two screens according to keyboard keys

1924–1925	Hosts Boy Scout Radio Program initially for KFWB in Hollywood	George Gerswhin's *Rhapsody in Blue* premiered (1924); Pierre Boulez born (1925)
1927		First talking picture, *The Jazz Singer*, premiered
1928	Graduated Los Angeles High School, valedictorian; enters Pomona State College	*An American in Paris* premiered
1930	Travels in Europe; studies art	
1931	Returns to California; remains until mid-1933	*Three Places in New England* by Charles Ives premiered
1933	Travels to New York; meets Henry Cowell	*Ionisation* by Edgard Varèse premiered; Arnold Schoenberg arrives in U.S., never returning to Germany
1934	Returns to California; studies with Schoenberg	*Four Saints in Three Acts* by Virgil Thomson and Gertrude Stein premiered
1935	Marries Xenia Andreyevna Kashevaroff	Alban Berg dies
1937	Works as dance accompanist at UCLA and Mills College; composes music for Sylvilla Fort's *Bacchanale* for prepared piano	Premier of Carl Orff's *Carmina Burana*; demise of Charles-Marie Widor, the lone surviving pupil of Rossini and teacher of three generations of French composers

1938	Works as dance accompanist at Cornish School of the Arts; meets Merce Cunningham	
1939–1945		World War II
1939	Moves to San Francisco; works with Lou Harrison on percussion pieces	Invention of the Vocoder, first electronic instrument to reproduce human voice; first permance of Charles Ives's Second Piano Sonata, titled *Concord, Mass. 1840–1860*
1940		World premiere of Schoenberg's *Violin Concerto*, written in 1936, a seminal twelve-tone work
1941	Moves to Chicago	Marcel Duchamp returns to New York and settles in the city for the remainder of his life
1942	Moves to New York; music for *Credo in Us* (dance by Cunningham)	
1943	Percussion Ensemble concert at Museum of Modern Art	New York Philharmonic conducting debut of Leonard Bernstein; premiers of Darius Milhaud's *Opus Americanum*, Leonard Herrmann's *For the Fallen*, Marc Blitzstein's *Freedom Morning*, and Aaron Copland's *Fanfare for the Common Man*
1944		*Appalachian Spring* by Aaron Copland, with choreography

1944 (cont.)	by Martha Graham, premieres; Merce Cunningham appearing as the Preacher
1945 Divorced; begins study of Eastern philosophy under D. T. Suzuki	Deaths of Pietro Mascagni (b. 1863), the Italian opera composer, Anton von Webern (b. 1884), the Viennese dodecaphonist; and Béla Bartók (b. 1881), the Hungarian "explorer in his symphonic and chamber music of the outermost frontiers of long rhythms and dynamic nuances, indefatigable collector and codifier of ethnically diversified folksong" (to quote Nicolas Slonimsky)
1947 *The Seasons* premieres in New York	
1948 Teaches at Black Mountain College	Early commercial tape recorders introduced in the United States, replacing wire transcription
1949 *Sonatas and Interludes for Prepared Piano* premiered	First LP introduced by Columbia
1950	Pierre Schaeffer and Pierre Henry introduce *musique concrète* in Paris
1952 *Music of Changes* premiered; composes first piece for tape, *Imaginary Landscape No. 5*; *4'33"* premiered; *Williams Mix* for tape	"Closed circuit" live Metropolitan Opera performance of Bizet's *Carmen* on the screens of thirty-one music houses in twenty-seven American cities; first public concert of tape recorder music composed by Otto Luening and Vladimir

		Ussachevsky; premiere of Marc Blitzstein's Americanized adaptation of Kurt Weill's *Threepenny Opera*
1953		Karlheinz Stockhausen's *Electronic Study No. 1*
1954	Moves to Rockland County artist's colony	Charles Ives dies
1955		*Target with Four Faces* by Jasper Johns
1956	Teaches first class at New School for Social Research	Ampex introduces eight-track recording machinery; Elvis Presley hits the charts
1958	Twenty-five year retrospective concert; *Fontana Mix*	Van Cliburn, Louisiana-born (1934), Texas-bred, cops top prize at Tchaikovsky competition in Moscow; death at 84 of W. C. Handy, "the father of the blues"
1959	*Indeterminacy* recorded with David Tudor	*Broadcast* by Robert Rauschenberg
1961	*Silence* published; *Atlas Eclipticalis*	Yuri Gagarin, a young Soviet cosmonaut, sings a Dmitry Shostakovich song, serenading outer space with earthly voice for the first time
1962		The Beatles make their first recording; Moog synthesizer first introduced; *Ice Cream Cone* by Claes Oldenburg
1963		*Available Forms I* by Earle Brown premieres in New York; *Pop Art* show opens at

1963 (*cont.*)		Museum of Modern Art, launching the careers of Andy Warhol and Robert Rauschenberg
1964		*Ensembles for Synthesizers* by Milton Babbitt; *In C* by Terry Riley
1965	*Rozart Mix*	Henry Cowell dies
1967	*A Year from Monday*	*Switched on Bach* by Walter Carlos, first commercially successful recording featuring Moog synthesizer
1968		*Rainforest,* with choreography by Merce Cunningham and a score by Gordon Mumma and David Tudor, premieres; Marcel Duchamp dies
1969	*HPSCHD* premiere; edited *Notations*; produced *Not Wanting to Say Anything About Marcel*	Woodstock Music Festival The temporary "radicalization" of American universities
1970	*Song Books; Mureau;* Richard Kostelanetz's *John Cage: A Documentary Monograph*	The Beatles break up
1971	*62 Mesostics re Merce Cunningham*	Stravinksy and Louis Armstrong die
1972	*Cheap Imitations*	First performance of Kirk Nurock's Natural Sound Workshop
1974	Composes *Etudes Astrales* based on astrological charts	IRCAM, an electronic music laboratory, is launched in Paris by Pierre Boulez

1976		*Einstein on the Beach* by Philip Glass and Robert Wilson
1977		3M introduces first digital recording machines
1978	*Writings Through Finnegans Wake*	Judy Chicago's *The Dinner Party,* an installation on feminist themes
1979	*Roaratorio*	Premiere of of Alan Hovhaness's Thirty-Sixth Symphony
1982	Cage's 70th birthday; Wall to Wall Cage festival presented at Symphony Space	*Koyaanisqatsi* soundtrack by Philip Glass; deaths of pianists Glenn Gould (b. 1932), Thelonius Monk (b. 1919), and Artur Rubenstein (b. 1887)
1985	*ASLSP* for piano	*Piano Concerto* by Lou Harrison premiered by Keith Jarrett
1986	*Etcetera 2/4 Orchestra*	Premiere of Alan Hovhaness's Symphony No. 60, *To the Appalachian Mountains*
1987	*Europera 1 & 2*	Premiere of John Adams' *Nixon in China*
1988	*I–VI* (Norton lectures at Harvard)	Death of eccentric and controversial composers Giacinto Scelsi (b. 1905) and Kaikhosru Sorabji (b. 1892 as Leon Dudley)
1989	*Europera 3 & 4*	Death of tunesmith Irving Berlin (b. 1888), the African singer known as Franco (b. 1938), the the pianist Vladimir Horowitz (b. 1893), and the British composer Lennox Berkeley (b. 1903)

1991	*Europera 5*	*Beachbirds* choreography by Merce Cunningham, with music by Cage
1992	Dies at home	Deaths of French composer Oliver Messiaen (b. 1908) and international actress Marlene Dietrich (b. 1903)
1993	*Rolyholyover*	

Index